EXPECT the LIGHT!

Expect the Light!

Gene Shelburne

 COLLEGE PRESS
PUBLISHING COMPANY
Joplin, Missouri

Cover Design by Mark A. Cole

Although the events are real, the names and other details in
some of these stories have been changed for the purpose of
protecting the people depicted and/or their families.

Library of Congress Cataloging-in-Publication Data

Shelburne, Gene, 1939–
    Expect the light!/Gene Shelburne.
       p.   cm.
    ISBN 0-89900-790-2 (pbk.)
       1. Suffering—Religious aspects—Christianity—Case
studies.   2. Christian biography—United States   I. Title.
BT732.7.S44 1997
248.8'6—dc21   97-20049
                                                              CIP

Contents

morning when she stepped into my study. How can Christians cope with the loss of dignity that so often goes with advancing years?

If you were locked up in a dangerous prison for a crime you didn't do, would you think God put you there?

Unfinished walls spoke starkly of dreams now dead. But in God's good light the builder's widow still saw His glory.

Less than a week before Christmas, Rusty Barnett's wife died suddenly, leaving him and a houseful of kids. How do you hold a funeral like that? At Christmas?

Jan Thomas thought her life ended the day her husband left her and the kids to move in with his Sweet-Young-Thing. But God touched her with his grace, providing new strength and reviving her hope. How did this happen?

"In this hope we are saved," the Bible says. I always wondered what that meant until I watched my mother dying.

Like the brilliant leaves of autumn, life is fragile. Frighteningly so.

Saralynn waited too late to face the truth about her wife-abusing husband. Even in her darkest days, however, she found light in God's word.

A sad little man invited himself to dinner with me that day. To live with his loneliness, though, he needed more than me.

When his dear wife, Muriel, was stricken with Alzheimer's, Dr. Robertson McQuilkin walked away from a career many would covet to care for her. Celebrate with these good people the victory of their faith and love.

Preface: Breaking Through

We awoke that Wednesday to a dark, gray, sloppy day, the pre-dawn darkness dulled by a mix of rain, snow, and dust. Snust, I guess you'd call it. Clouds were low and lowering. Wind-swept fog and mist whipped against our windshield as we hurried to catch a much-too-early flight.

We were glad our plane had spent the night in Amarillo. It could not have landed in this morning's murky soup. Sensible geese were grounded. "Would the pilot try to take off?" we wondered. He did.

Taxiing through puddles, he followed the runway lines and lights in haze that often obscured the hangars and buildings on the airport's fringe.

Finally came the familiar thrust and we began a dash into the darkness. The plane's nose tilted upward, tugging the frantic wheels loose from the saturated earth, and we hurtled heavenward into the seemingly impenetrable clouds.

The darkness that had cloaked the earth below instantly swallowed the silver plane. As we plunged ever deeper into its entrails, cut off from God above and humanity below it seemed in that surreal moment, the knotted intestines of the angry cloud bank wallowed past the windows as if it were trying to digest its latest morsel.

Suddenly, however, we escaped its grasp. Out of the gloom we soared into a luminous whiteness that lit the plane's interior brighter than a thousand lights, and then, in a breathtaking instant, we broke free. Into the crystal clarity of open sky with the radiant just-risen sun infusing the endless terrain of cottony cloud tops with indomitable brightness.

Thus, in an early morning hour, we reenacted the usual cycle of life. The daunting trek through darkness followed, however unexpectedly, by a reemergence into light. Grief gives way to gladness. Death makes way for life. "Sorrow tarries for the night," God says, "but joy comes in the morning."

The secret of survival lies in an unshakable faith that even when the clouds of life are darkest, the sun of God's grace shines undimmed above. And we know at any moment, perhaps soon, we will bask once more in its warmth and glory.

To make it through today, expect the light.

Mary's Shame

Near the cross of Jesus stood his mother, his mother's sister, Mary the wife of Clopas, and Mary Magdalene. When Jesus saw his mother there, and the disciple whom he loved standing nearby, he said to his mother, "Dear woman, here is your son," and to the disciple, "Here is your mother." From that time on, this disciple took her into his home (John 19:25-27).

I'm convinced that the resurrection can provide a woman new light on her role as a mother.

Let me explain what I mean.

"This fellow was a brother to Jesus, too." I pointed to the name of Jude in the list of the authors of what we usually call "The General Letters" in the New Testament.

"Just like James?" One of my students indicated the Bible book name at the top of the list on the chalkboard.

"That's right," I praised her. "Remember the list of Jesus' brothers we ran into way back in Mark's Gospel:

'James, Joseph, Simon, and Judas'?" These high school kids had been studying the New Testament with me in their credit Bible course every school day for several months. Now the semester was drawing to an end and I was delighted to see how much they had retained.

"Since Jesus' own brothers didn't even believe in him during his lifetime," I asked the kids, "does it surprise you to find two of them in this list of Bible authors?"

Several students nodded, and we began together to recall times in our Lord's ministry when members of his family were embarrassed by him. Mark tells us, for example, that when Jesus' family first heard about the huge crowds his miracles were drawing, "they went to take charge of him, for they said, 'He is out of his mind'" (3:21). He was becoming a family disgrace, they thought. John tells us that Jesus' brothers taunted him one year about going to the Feast of Tabernacles. In effect, they dared him to take his "sideshow" to the big crowds in Jerusalem and there to display the miracle powers they didn't believe in.

"Well, it would be hard to believe that your own brother was God's Son," one perceptive girl in the class piped up. Picturing the problem in terms of her own siblings, she mused, "After you played marbles or rode to New Mexico with a kid, how could you worship him as your Lord or honor him as your King?"

"That's right, Dorie," I agreed. "So," I turned to the whole class, "what convinced James and Jude and the other brothers that this lad they grew up with really was somebody special?"

"His resurrection," they all answered.

"But what about Mary?" one of my sharpest girls asked, wrinkling her face as she wrestled with the newness of the thought. "Mary knew how Jesus was born. Why would she show up with her other boys to try to get him to come home? She had to know who Jesus was. She knew he wasn't crazy. She believed in him all the way, didn't she?"

"Yes, Erin," I agreed. "She had to. But think about Mary's situation in Nazareth. Every old lady in town had counted up the months of her pregnancy." (On my knuckles I ticked off "January, February, March, April . . .") Everybody in town knew Jesus had been conceived before Mary and Joseph said 'I do.' In their eyes Jesus was illegitimate, and Mary had been a bad girl. That was over 30 years ago, but in first-century Palestine that kind of shame never went away. So you can understand, can't you, why Mary would want her oldest son to maintain a low profile? Every new tale of a leper cleansed or a demon cast out fueled the local gossip and deepened the family's stigma. For Mary it would have been much easier if Jesus had just come home and made sawdust in the carpenter's shop. His fame increased her pain."

Our class discussion was interrupted by the bell. But I think most of those high school youngsters, especially the girls, left class that day with a new appreciation of Mary and the price she paid to be a mother.

Gladly Paying the Price

Every mother pays a price. And not just the costs we all expect, like dirty diapers and 2 a.m. feedings. Because of her part in the Eden fiasco, God told Eve, "I will greatly increase your pains in childbearing; with pain you will give birth to children" (Genesis 3:16). But the pain of mothering only starts there. Sigmund Freud theorized that the trauma of birth leaves lifelong mental stretch marks on every baby's psyche, so he reasoned that most weird behavior can be traced back to the violent way all of us enter this world. I think he overlooked the fact that the person affected most deeply and most lastingly by the pain of childbirth is not the child but the mother. In every case. "A foolish son brings grief to his mother," the Proverbs tell us. The truth is that *all* children bring some grief to their mothers. It goes with the territory. And most mothers bear it gladly.

On Mother's Day, 1968, Velma Shepard received a telegram from the Department of Defense telling her that her picture-perfect son Ronnie had been killed in action in Vietnam. Only God knows how many tears this Christian mother has shed because of that loss, but I think Velma would tell you without hesitation that the blessings of being loved by a son like Ronnie far outweigh any tears he cost her.

As longtime Christian friend Tom Edwards and I were chatting this week, he launched into a tale that somehow involved his daughter's messy divorce. Tom's eyes misted as the hurt of the situation bludgeoned his heart for the umpteenth time. He glanced up at me and asked, "You haven't been there yet, have you?" Six years after that daughter's divorce, Tom and his wife Jean still spend lots of dollars and lots of hours on damage control for that girl. And for the grandkids. For Tom and Jean these have been hard years filled with way too much pain, but if Jean had a choice, I assure you that she would gladly give birth to that daughter again.

Mothers are like that. Strangely enough it seems that the more we cost them in heartache and strain, the more they love us. Repeatedly we observe that the more troubled and troublesome the child, the more intense the mother's love. A stranger would turn away in disgust, but not a mother. It's the son in prison, the daughter with chronic mental illness, the 30-year-old who's always up to his ears in debt, the alcoholic, the one who is crippled, or the one with severe learning disabilities who most totally captures a mother's heart. She loves all her kids, but the one in trouble demands more prayer, more encouragement, more attention in every way. Therefore the mother bonds more urgently with that son or daughter. You've seen this phenomenon, haven't you? Maybe it's going on right now in your own home.

My own mother played this role, and for several years I was the child who attracted a disproportionate share of her maternal affections. About the time I was turning five, I awakened her night after night sobbing because my legs ached. "Maybe it's growing pains," the family doctor guessed, but for weeks the nighttime pain disrupted my mother's sleep and mine. Finally another doctor in a clinic miles from our home diagnosed rheumatic fever. The next seven months I spent in bed. I didn't realize at the time that my illness dictated the whole family's schedule (how do you go to the ballpark or on a picnic or on a vacation when one of your kids can't get out of bed?). My illness changed the entire family's menu. My doctoring deflated the family's already tight budget. Looking back, however, I now realize that the greatest impact my bout with rheumatic fever had on our family was the way it consumed my mother's energy and focused her anxiety. Not just while I was sick, but for years to come.

Long after I was up and out of bed, Mom remembered the old doctor's strong warnings that they needed to limit my activities, lest my weakened heart be damaged. So Mom watched me. Closely. Much more closely than probably is healthy for either a son or a mother. Imagine her anxiety four years later when I came running into the house all excited one afternoon to tell her I had just been hired to run a paper route. All the way across town. At 5 o'clock every morning. Imagine her fears when I even mentioned participating in school sports. Every job I accepted, every activity I attempted aroused her exaggerated maternal fears. I was 20 years old when I signed on to do heavy construction work for Southwestern Public Service. I still remember the worried look in her eyes. She never believed the company doctor who certified me to be fit for such labor.

That's the price my own mother paid to be a mother. I cost her years of escalated worry. While I love her for it, I really don't think she was all that unusual in her response. Most mothers turn up their mothering instincts an extra notch or two when one of their offspring is in trouble. Most of them do it willingly, without complaint. "No man takes my life from me," Jesus said. "I lay it down of my own accord." That's how good mothers almost always respond when one of their children encounters distress.

Look at Mary at the foot of the cross. Watch her as she ignores the danger, embraces the sorrow, bears the pain. When her son needs her most, she is there for him. Regardless of what it might cost her. Because of women like her, today we honor mothers.

It's even more interesting, though, to look at Mary *after* the cross. After the resurrection, Romans 1 tells us,

Jesus was "declared to be the Son of God by his resurrection from the dead." Mary is probably the only person who did not need that confirmation. She knew for sure that Jesus was God's Son. Only after the resurrection did her own children — men like Bible writers James and Jude — change their unspoken evaluation of their mama's early behavior. Until now they had quietly assumed that their mother got in bed with Joseph a few months too early. Now, in the light of the open tomb, Mary's motherhood was vindicated.

I suggest to you that Mary is not the only mother who has lived under a cloud and waited long, hard years for her motherhood to be affirmed. Those who know the story of Winston Churchill know he had major problems in his school days. His poor mother was summoned to more than one disciplinary session. Young Winston simply did not like school, and his schoolmasters didn't think much of him either. He was an educational terror. I don't know Churchill's story well enough to say, but I hope his mother lived long enough to see his election as Prime Minister of England. I hope she lived long enough to see him courageously lead the free world to victory over Hitler's Nazi forces, so she could hold her head high and proclaim, "That's my boy!" If she did, she understood Mary's joy after the resurrection.

In the same era in Italy a peasant woman, hardly able to provide food for her family, still slaved to pay for her ten-year-old's voice lessons. One impatient teacher turned away the boy, saying, "You can't sing. Your voice sounds like wind in the shutters." Mama kept struggling to develop the talent she saw in her youngster, sometimes even going without shoes in order to pay the cost of his training. The hard days of poverty and insult were forgotten when the entire world one day acclaimed Enrico Caruso as the greatest singer of his generation. Like Mary, his mother lived to see her faith vindicated.

In a mid-sized Kansas town Greg Wilson manages a White's Auto Store. Years ago in junior high school, Greg started running with a wild crew and began boozing. Beer gave way to marijuana in high school. Cocaine was the natural progression in college. By the time he was a young adult his widowed mother was heartbroken to have raised a kid who couldn't hold a job or stay in school. She prayed and wept and wondered where she had failed.

Right when the situation seemed most hopeless Greg met a fine lady. He didn't know it at the time, but later he confessed that he was attracted to her by the same qualities of faith and decency and goodness that he once scorned in his own mother. At the low point of his life his mother's goodness was the influence that nudged his life back on course. Greg married this upright woman and did a 180-degree turn in lifestyle. It's not exaggerating to say Greg Wilson was resurrected. That's how the Bible describes it. Greg was "buried with Christ" and "raised to newness of life." Now he is "dead to sin and alive to God through Jesus Christ." And Greg's mother, like Mary, once more holds her head high, her mothering validated by a resurrected son.

If one of your children today is misguided and in trouble, good Mother, don't despair. We are the people who believe in resurrection. Hold on to that faith and don't be undone by today's darkness.

Expect the light.

Life Without Hope

We always thank God, the Father of our Lord Jesus Christ, when we pray for you, because we have heard of your faith in Christ Jesus and of the love you have for all the saints — the faith and love that spring from the hope that is stored up for you in heaven and that you have already heard about in the word of truth, the gospel that has come to you. All over the world this gospel is bearing fruit and growing, just as it has been doing among you since the day you heard it and understood God's grace in all its truth (Colossians 1:1-6).

Nobody ever conjured up a more elaborate picture of hell than Dante. In his famous work *The Inferno* he takes his readers on a grand tour of the Underworld with all its horrors and hellishness. But in five short words Dante gave a much simpler description of the realm of Satan when he wrote, "Life without hope is hell."

I understand Dante's words better because I knew Jack Bickly. Let me tell you about him.

For years Jack earned his bread as an electrical contractor. A towering Teddy bear of a man, Jack showed up at our church whenever the doors were opened for worship or study. Jack had been reared in the Texas panhandle by staunch Christian parents. He followed in their righteous footsteps of faith and basic integrity. In the early days of my ministry in Amarillo, I was always pleased when Jack stopped by the church to pass the time of day. His perpetual smile lit up my study. His tales about his latest job always added interest to my day. Several times I closed my books, hopped into his old truck, and puttered around town with Jack as he gathered up materials from several junked semi-trailers he used to warehouse his supplies.

During those days I got to know Jack pretty well. I found out how hard he was struggling to make a living in a time when Amarillo's air base had just closed and our area's economy had bottomed out. I found out how much he adored both his only child, and the lady who had borne him that talented daughter. Bit by bit Jack let me inside his private thoughts enough for me to know the consternation that stirred his soul because of changes he was seeing in the way the church sounded and acted in those post-Kennedy days. Things he thought had been set in concrete turned out to be floating and flexible. Sometimes the changes made him angry. Sometimes they left him puzzled. Because the church mattered so much to Jack, no shift in her work or worship was neutral. He had to analyze every change in the light of the Scriptures, and sometimes what he saw didn't seem to fit what he read. At least, not the way he read it. So we talked. A lot. Sometimes loudly. As Jack struggled to be true to his faith.

I don't think I'm talking out of school when I tell you that Jack had a temper. Everybody knew it. I didn't see him lose his more than a time or two. I'd heard about it from others who had been present when he had gone ballistic. Maybe his family or his employees felt the fury of his wrath more often than I realized, but I doubt it. When Jack did blow his stack, it was such a monumental happening that the tale was widely told, but his legendary anger became less intimidating to me when I saw that Jack seldom was angry at people. Instead he got furious about circumstances he considered intolerable (things like sloppy work on the job, or unexpected innovations at church), but Jack was basically benevolent toward people. He liked people and never meant to hurt anybody when his temper flared. Almost instantly he seemed to be sorry if anybody got wounded by his words, and he was quick to say so. Realizing this made me more sympathetic to the strong feelings that stirred inside this big man.

I have always wondered what part Jack's anger played in his stroke. In the early '80s Jack closed his contracting business and went to work for the city as an electrical inspector. It seemed like a job perfectly suited to his skills, and his smiling, affable nature surely must have helped him get along with the builders when he prowled their job sites. Jack stayed so busy on this new job that we didn't get to visit like we did in earlier days, but he seemed to be enjoying an 8-to-5 job without the never-ending pressures that go along with running your own business. Anyway, I was shocked when the call came to tell me Jack had gotten sick on the job and had been hospitalized with what appeared to be a stroke.

For days Jack hovered between life and death. The

stroke had been a bad one. He couldn't talk, or walk, or control his arms or fingers. Jack lay encased in his immense, immobile body, a prisoner inside his own unresponsive flesh, able to communicate in those first days only by blinking his eyes. When speech returned, he sounded like a drunk man slurring indecipherable syllables into patterns previously unheard by human ears. Patiently he would repeat himself over and over, until somebody in the room guessed what he was saying. Then he would flash a wacky looking uncontrolled smile and begin to nod his head excitedly, almost as if it were a game.

"I'm going home by summer," Jack assured me one day in his distorted drawl. Every day for Jack was filled with intense physical therapy, therapy that obviously was doing some good. Every time I visited him he was eager to show off some new muscular skill. Still he could not stand or walk, but his left arm and right fingers were beginning to move at his command. They ordered a special motorized wheelchair for him, one he could control with his left hand, or with his mouth. Jack had visions of riding through the front door of his home in that fancy wheelchair, and he talked often of "going home." I could tell that his highly skilled therapists were spurring his efforts toward recovery by fanning in Jack a growing hope that he would soon return home.

The "summer" in Jack's dreams turned into "September" when his physical gains plateaued. Still he worked hard, intent on the goal of going home to Hawthorne Street. But you can't go home when your right arm doesn't know it's yours and your legs act like you dialed the wrong area code. I watched sadly as Jack's bright hopes began to fade. The nurses stopped

putting him into the high-tech wheelchair. He never
gained enough muscular coordination to control it. His
therapists tried to "let him down" gently, but how do
you cushion the hard reality that the home you're going
to is not your own residence? It's a nursing home.
Where you're surrounded by pitiful people who long
ago lost all hope of going anywhere better. Now you lie
looking at the same ceiling day after day. Unable to turn
your own body. Unable to care for your own physical
needs. And each day, without therapists to challenge
and cheer you, the meager muscle tone you gained in
those arduous hours of therapy slips away.

And with it, your hope.

✳ ✳ ✳ ✳ ✳

Years ago, when I first made a serious study of Paul's
letter to the Colossian church, the beginning verses of
this letter piqued my curiosity. Three things the apostle
complimented these new Christians for (it seems he was
always complimenting his converts, wasn't he?). He told
them he was impressed by their faith. All over the broth-
erhood people were talking about how strong they were
in the Lord. He also praised them for their love that had
blessed other Christians in many places. Faith and love
were qualities I expected Paul to recognize and encourage in these brand new followers of Jesus, but I was
surprised by the third thing he singled out for commen-
dation: their hope. It never had occurred to me to
compliment anybody because of their hope.

But I must confess that I was a young man then.
Maybe a guy in his early 20s hasn't lived enough, or cried
enough, or lost enough to know the preciousness of hope.
Most of us at that age have never been without it, so we

don't recognize the devastation suffered by souls who despair. Dante was right. "Life without hope is hell."

That's why the days right after the divorce decree becomes final are so depressing. Until then, we nurse a futile hope that somehow, some way the relationship might be rekindled, the marriage saved. Now it's over.

That's why the bottom falls out and anger kicks in when the doctor says, "I'm sorry. Your cancer is untreatable. There's nothing more we can do."

That's why permanent disabilities are so much harder to deal with than temporary illnesses. Without hope, it's hard to cope.

My best buddy in high school wrote me recently. "I'm not a Christian," he said, "but I try to live like one." Indeed he does. He's always been a clean living, decent guy. A true friend with a keen sense of truth and fairness. I'm sure he's a fine husband to his Christian wife, and a great father for his two children. Professionally, he's the best. He probably lives more "like a Christian" than many Christians do. Without buying into our faith, my friend still can be a sterling fellow, but the one thing he cannot reproduce without faith is the Christian's hope in dark times. When the world crashes around his ears (as it will for all of us one day), where can he look for light? Brilliant man that he is, my friend still cannot say with T.S. Eliot, "In my end is my beginning." His failure to believe cuts him off from this ultimate hope. While life is good, and health is whole, and the sun shines brightly on the meadow, this may not seem to matter. But where can my friend find hope when his days grow dark?

"If in this life only we have hope," the Bible warns, "we are of all men most miserable."

✳ ✳ ✳ ✳ ✳

Confined for years in a second-rate nursing home bed, trapped with smells and sounds most of us can't wait to get away from, Jack Bickly taught us the true meaning of hope. When they took from him all expectation of physical improvement, Jack's faith fastened onto a more substantial hope — his unshakable trust in an unseeable God. "Hope stored up for you in the heavens," Paul called it when he wrote to the Colossians. Hope that, according to him, all of us should learn about in the gospel. Lying there year after year in that stinking, depressing nursing home, Jack showed us the kind of faith and love and hope Paul commended in the Christians of Colossae.

In this respect we Christians are really no different from the unbelieving friend I just alluded to. It's not hard for us to appear strong and loving and hopeful when life is pleasant and all goes well. Hoping is easy when we're surrounded by visible reasons to be hopeful. But true faith enables us to hang on to hope when all reasons for hope have vanished. Like ancient Abraham, "against hope" the true believer "in hope continues to believe" (Romans 4:18). If this seems like nonsense, just look at Jack Bickly and explain to me how else a man in that condition could continue to be loving and grateful and pleasant. How he could continue to act like he had a reason to be, when the rest of us had trouble seeing it. It is this unseeable hope, hope that goes against and beyond tangible, visible circumstances, that we gain when we truly set our hope on the risen Christ. When I see hope like this in a fellow like Jack Bickly, I begin to think it may be the truest mark of genuine faith.

Our world is hungry for this kind of hope. Foolishly our generation staked its hopes on advances in human knowledge and invention. One of the most challenging books I've read in recent years is Leonard Allen's *The Cruciform Church*. Allen is right when he says that in the past two or three decades "technology dazzled the mind with the rush of comforts, conveniences, and cures." It looked for a brief moment like we were headed for heaven on earth. But while we were making all these fabulous improvements, Allen laments, "Alienation, global violence, despair, and suicide seemed to keep pace."

Short on hope, this generation turns to cocaine and gangs and mindless mayhem. Without hope it seeks relief in addictions and divorce and unholy indulgences of every sort. Those who abandon faith are doomed to live "life with a lid" — life with no dimension beyond the agony and distress of the present moment. With no God to rescue. No heaven to get ready for. In other words, life with no hope.

For ten years Jack Bickly was a quadriplegic, almost completely paralyzed from the neck down. Those of us who looked in on Jack from time to time were delighted by unexpected improvements in his situation. After several years in a care center that left a lot to be desired, Jack was allowed to move into the fine new long-term care facility at the Veteran's Hospital. The quality of his care improved immensely, his living conditions were infinitely better.

"Look at this!" he beamed at me one Sunday afternoon. From beneath the cover, without anybody's help, he extracted his left arm and waved it in a semi-controlled sweep above his bed.

"When did you learn to do that?" I yelped as I dodged his flying hand.

"Oh, they work with me everyday," Jack smiled proudly. "I spend time in therapy every morning."

"Well, they're obviously doing you some good," I praised him.

"You bet!" Jack agreed. And then he confided, "If I keep improving at this rate, they tell me I could be home by Christmas!"

✸ ✸ ✸ ✸ ✸

Jack made it. Before daybreak one August morning nurses found his abandoned body on the hospital bed. Jack had gone home.

When the Road Darkens

Out of the heartaches of his own life, the popular English fantasy writer J.R.R. Tolkien drew some keen insights to share with the readers of his fairy tales.

Tucked away deep in *The Fellowship of the Ring*, for example, his readers may happen upon this marvelous exchange:

"Faithless is he that says farewell when the road darkens," said Gimli.

"Maybe," said Elrond, "but let him not vow to walk in the dark, who has not seen the nightfall."

Tolkien had "seen the nightfall." Many who offer cheap comfort and quick advice have not. They have never even glimpsed the darkness. "I know what you're going through" can be the cruelest words on the human tongue when spoken by a person who obviously has never been there.

In our efforts to console the sufferers around us, we can come off sounding like the young preacher who recently asserted (with a positiveness reserved for young preachers only) that divorce is always wrong and remarriage forever disqualifies one for service in God's kingdom. He has not yet wept through the agony of marital failure with someone he really loves.

"Through much tribulation you must enter the kingdom," Paul taught his converts.

Only through suffering do we earn admission to the hearts of those who also hurt. When we have looked at the world through tears, perhaps then we might dare to comment on the perspective of friends who are crying.

Many of us have seen the nightfall. We have known the fear of sudden illness, the panic of undiagnosed pain. We have laid our loved ones to rest, but not our hearts. We have wept when our children made mistakes, and when we made worse ones.

Thank God, we also have seen the Light, who alone can help us when darkness invades our souls.

Out of the Darkness

There will be no more gloom for those who were in distress. In the past he humbled the land of Zebulun and the land of Naphtali, but in the future he will honor Galilee of the Gentiles, by the way of the sea, along the Jordan — The people walking in darkness have seen a great light; on those living in the land of the shadow of death a light has dawned (Isaiah 9:1-2).

Originally it was told as a true story.

Since truth is often stranger than fiction, it may have been true. But the tale has been told so many times by so many tellers that it has grown, no doubt, with all the subtle twists and inevitable adornments various story-tellers have tagged on. Not meaning to falsify. Just noticing in passing what seem to be obvious inferences from the story's core content. Thus each teller of the tale has embellished it. As I also am likely to when I repeat it now for you.

The events in this story had to have happened some time in the early Sixties. In Nyack, New York, we're

told. When Dr. H.P. Chase was pastor of the First
Reformed Church there.

In the weeks right before Christmas the church had
suffered some damage from a fierce Atlantic storm. The
old roof over their sanctuary leaked during the gale.
Plaster on the wall alongside the pulpit got soaked.
When it dried and crumbled, the resulting damage left
an unsightly crater, but workmen said they were
swamped. They couldn't even begin repairs until the
holidays were past. So Dr. Chase had resigned himself
to preaching "Peace on Earth" that year in a setting that
looked like it had been strafed and bombed.

Then, at least so it seemed to this good pastor, the
Lord provided. Early in December the church ladies
held a rummage sale. An auction. To support their
ministry to homeless children in some distant land.
Toward the end of the sale, the auctioneer opened
bidding for a fancy gold tablecloth. The huge linen was
uniquely embroidered, much too ornate to risk at any
normal meal. And the cloth was far too large to fit an
average home dining table. When nobody showed any
interest in this usual item, Dr. Chase had a brainstorm
that made him smile. Bidding what he had in his pocket
— $6.20, he purchased the swath of golden fabric and
set about at once to hang it as a tapestry on the front
wall of the sanctuary. It was perfect. It just covered the
unsightly holes.

Two weeks later, with Christmas only days away,
winter came again to Nyack with a vengeance. Sleet
sliced across the gray morning sky, like shrapnel, driven
by bone-chilling winds from the sea. Outside his study
window at the church Dr. Chase could see a bus bench.
As he watched, an older woman sat down on the bench,

all bundled up against the ice and wind. She had no way to know that the bus had just come by and the next one was not due for almost an hour. Fearing for her safety in the storm, the pastor called to her from the church door and invited her to wait inside where it was warm. She accepted gladly.

As she stepped inside the little church, she greeted the pastor in broken English, and he returned her greeting with a smile. "What are you doing out on a nasty day like this?" he inquired.

"Oh, I've just answered an ad for a job. But they turned me down. My English is not good enough, they said." As she told her tale of that day's woe, her eyes fastened on the gold cloth hanging on the sanctuary wall. Stepping near, she ran her fingers over the embroidery in amazement. "Pastor," she said to Dr. Chase, her eyes shining with excitement, "this cloth once was mine."

"Really?"

"When my husband and I lived in Vienna, we travelled to Brussels on holiday not long before the war. While we were there, he bought me this cloth for the large table in our formal dining room. Then the Nazis came. In 1942 they hauled away my husband to the concentration camps where so many died. I never saw him again."

"In that case," Dr. Chase said at once, "I will take down the tapestry and give it back to you. It should still be yours."

"Oh, no!" the woman objected. "I have no place for such a fine cloth anymore. Besides, it makes me happy to know that God and his people are using it."

Dr. Chase and his new friend chatted for awhile.

Then she put on her coat and scarf again and, with the pastor's holiday greetings warming her heart, she ventured back out into the cold just in time to catch her bus.

On Christmas Eve a band of people from the neighborhood filled the church for the special evening of worship. When the service was over and the worshipers were leaving, an elderly watchmaker limped down the aisle toward the pulpit. Swimming upstream, as it were, against the departing crowd. "That cloth!" he said to the pastor. "That cloth! I've been studying it ever since the service began tonight. I'm sure it's the same one I gave to my wife in Brussels in 1942. We went home from there to Vienna, and soon afterward I was hauled away to a concentration camp." The half-bald, white-haired little man stood fingering the precious golden fabric as if he could rub memories out of the thread.

"I never saw my Emma again," he said, and bowed his head. "So many people in our district died in the war."

Hardly able to believe his ears, Dr. Chase told the watchmaker about the woman he had met only three days before. "I suppose she could be your wife, but how could we ever find her?"

In a four-day-old newspaper the minister found the ad for the job the woman had applied for. Although it was getting late now on Christmas Eve, he called the people who had placed the ad. Briefly he told them what had happened. "Is it possible that you still have the name and address of the woman you turned down because of her poor English?" Out of the trash can where they had tossed the application, these people retrieved the information.

On Christmas morning Dr. Chase and the watchmaker drove together to a small town almost 50 miles from Nyack and located the address they had been given the night before. They went up to the door and knocked. Dr. Chase stepped back and watched with wonder as a husband and wife who had been separated 20 years by the war and who had given each other up as dead were reunited that Christmas Day.

❋ ❋ ❋ ❋ ❋

It's a grand story, isn't it? One that will be retold over and over. As it should be.

But in the glow of its ending, let's not miss its truth. The watchmaker and his long-lost wife found each other again because of a storm. Because of broken plaster. Because a lady got turned down for a job. The disasters of the weeks before the holiday made possible the blessing of that Christmas Day. As so often happens when the hand of God is shaping our lives, *light came out of darkness*.

In fact, this seems to be God's favorite way of blessing us.

When Matthew the tax collector sat down to write the account of our Lord's earliest preaching and healing ministry in Galilee, he recalled two startling verses in Isaiah 9 that perfectly describe what happened. "Land of Zebulun and land of Naphtali, the way to the sea, along the Jordan, Galilee of the Gentiles," Isaiah begins, describing the same real estate four different ways just to be sure we know the location. What happens there in Galilee? Christ's ministry goes public, and — to use Isaiah's words — "the people living in darkness have seen a great light; on those living in the land of the shadow of death a light has dawned."

So often it happens like this when God's best blessings come our way. Darkness precedes his light.

It was that way for Joseph, wasn't it? Can you imagine a darker time in anybody's life than to be hauled
away from your family when you're just 17, and to be
sold on the slave market in a foreign land? I've often
wondered what went through Joseph's mind as he
trudged toward Egypt in chains. You and I know the
end of the story, of course. But he didn't. He had no
way to know that the slavers' chains, and the slander-
ous charges of a rich man's wife, and the years of
despair in Pharaoh's prison were God's way of getting
him ready for undreamed of glory. Only when he had
spent those years in darkness could Joseph bask in
God's glorious light.

In Bible days few men rose to greater honor than the
prophet Daniel. But his path to greatness led through a
dark valley of terror and tears. The armies of Babylon
swept through his land when Daniel was still a school-
boy. When they went home, they took with them Daniel
and dozens of other brilliant young students. Joseph left
home as a slave. Daniel was dragged away as a prisoner
of war. Can you imagine being held captive in central
Iraq? It wasn't much more fun then than now. Can you
imagine how homesick a boy like that must have been?
We go off to college for the first time, knowing we'll be
home for Christmas, and we almost die of homesick-
ness by mid-October. Daniel knew he would never go
home. But it took the darkness of those hard days to
prepare this fine young fellow for exalted service in the
limelight of all ages.

That's the sequence for God's blessings: darkness,
and then light.

It happened that way for so many people in the Gospels. Jairus had to know the anguish of a parent with a dying child, he had to taste the grief of one whose daughter died before he could witness the gift of Life. He came to the Lord's light through darkness.

So did Mary Magdalene. Would she ever have known the Lord's free love if she had not first been the tenement for seven devils? Would the leper have known the Savior's healing touch if he had somehow avoided the stigma and stench of the equivalence of AIDS in his day? If Lazarus had not died, he would never have heard his Friend and Master say, "Come forth!" He would have missed out on the miracle.

Over and over in the Gospels, it was the people who lived in darkness who saw the Light. Should we expect it to be any different for us today?

Think soberly about this, my friend, if today you are tempted to curse the darkness.

If loneliness and sadness shroud your soul these days and shut out all light —

If you've been ambushed by friends, so that betrayal and broken promises like arrows pierce your heart —

If your spirit is soggy from tears you've shed because a son or daughter has gone astray —

If troublesome addictions enslave your life and keep disrupting relationships that matter most to you —

If recent failures cloud your thinking and hide the sunlight of past success —

If pain and weakness fill your days, crowding out the joy and lightheartedness of times long past —

then I urge you to be aware that right now, as you sit in deep gloom and darkness, you are most likely to see the light of God.

I think this might be why Paul wrote, "We rejoice in our sufferings, because we know that suffering produces perseverance; perseverance, character; and character, hope. And hope does not disappoint us, because God has poured out his love into our hearts by the Holy Spirit, whom he has given us" (Romans 5:3-5).

This expectation of light out of darkness may explain the attitude that says, "Consider it pure joy, my brothers, whenever you face trials of many kinds, because you know that the testing of your faith develops perseverance. Perseverance must finish its work so that you may be mature and complete, not lacking anything" (James 1:2-4).

Don't misunderstand what I'm saying. Not for one instant would I wish upon any one of you the times of darkness that assail our souls. But I do want us to learn to recognize those dark times as the prelude to God's special goodness. I want us to claim the truth of the prophecy:

> *"The people walking in darkness*
> *have seen a great light!"*

Remember Calvary? Only when the sun had gone out, only when darkness covered that awful hill could the true greatness of the Lord Jesus shine forth. And it did shine. So brightly that his pagan murderer cried out, "Surely, this must be God's Son!"

We'll know him, too, when his light breaks through into the darkness of our lives.

5

Home at Last

They admitted that they were aliens and strangers on earth. People who say such things show that they are looking for a country of their own. If they had been thinking of the country they had left, they would have had opportunity to return. Instead, they were longing for a better country — a heavenly one. Therefore God is not ashamed to be called their God, for he has prepared a city for them (Hebrews 11:13b-16).

"I want to go home," the gray-haired lady in the hospital bed sobbed. "Why won't you just let me die? I want to go home."

"Mama, don't say that," her family scolded her. They couldn't stand to hear her candidly welcoming the death they dreaded. "Don't talk that way, Mama!" one of her daughters chided her. "You know you don't mean that."

But she did. With every fiber of her soul she yearned to go home. To be free from the indignity and anxiety of lingering, imminent death. Only in those rare moments when her death-denying family left her alone could I say to this good lady that I fully understood her longing to be released from the long months of weakness and pain and indignity. Only when they were out of her room could I pray with her for God to set her free from the cancer that had made a hell of her once happy and productive life.

Quietly I said to her, "I agree with you completely. It is past time for you to go home." She smiled and nodded. Before the week was past, God set her free.

✳ ✳ ✳ ✳ ✳

In almost four decades of ministry I have helped many people face death. Three hours ago I spoke words of comfort to the family of a young woman who seems to have gone home before her time. After a better-than-usual morning at work she hurried to her house to eat lunch. Before her soup got warm, her heart quit. They found her unexpectedly dead on her kitchen floor.

Life is temporary, I told the assembled mourners at that funeral. Life never was meant to last. The Bible speaks of us as "strangers and pilgrims" on the earth, I said. Most of the time we act like that isn't true. We spend most of our energy and time and money to do things and to acquire things that cannot last.

Face-to-face with death, reality jars us and we have to admit just how fragile and temporary we humans are. God is eternal. The Creator is permanent. But our created bodies simply won't last. They were not meant to last. The lady whose death we came to mourn was no exception to the most basic of all human statistics: one in one die.

Everything physical is vanishing, I reminded the funeral crowd. We buy a new car and it starts self-destructing before we make the final payment. Cars are physical; they vanish.

We purchase new clothes that make us feel so spiffy today, and three or four years later the same garments are threadbare and we're ashamed to be seen wearing them. Clothes are physical; they vanish.

We move into a new house we're so proud of, and to our dismay the place begins almost instantly to fall down. We can't patch things fast enough to keep up with the process of deterioration. Houses are physical; they vanish.

Our bodies are no different, we admitted beside that coffin today. In the hour when we are born our parents know already that we are destined for a grave. Everything physical vanishes.

So I reminded my fellow-mourners today of Jesus' warning, "Do not store up for yourselves treasures on earth, where moth and rust destroy, and where thieves break in and steal. But store up for yourselves treasures in heaven." And I shared Paul's evaluation: "If in this life only we have hoped, we are of all men most miserable" (1 Corinthians 15:19, RSV).

Why would I talk about such a morose subject at a funeral? Because I hoped that God would use that brief moment of stark reality, that eye-blink instant when God fully had our attention, to make us realize how confused we are when we begin to imagine that this present world is our home, that we really belong here.

God is getting us ready for an existence far more wonderful than anything we can dream of. At gut-level most of us know this, I think, but funerals seem to be one of the few times in life when we actually operate on that level.

"I consider that our present sufferings are not worth comparing with the glory that will be revealed in us," the apostle Paul said at a tough time in his life. He made it through the crisis by looking beyond today's pain to an eternity in God's heaven. Like many a soldier in the muck and misery of a brutal war, Paul was able to do his duty faithfully and patiently despite heartache and hardship because he knew he was on the way home.

The Homing Instinct

In one of the old spirituals we sing, "This world is not my home, I'm just a-passin' through." God put something deep inside each of us to make us yearn for home.

"Thou hast made us for Thee," St. Augustine wrote in his diary, "and we are restless until we come to Thee."

We are like salmon, who most of their days are content to feed and breed and swim in oceans and lakes hundreds, even thousands, of miles from the tiny streams where they were spawned. But the day comes when powerful urges drive the majestic creatures northward to their birthplace, and then no place will do but home.

We are like the Monarch butterflies, who all summer long flutter mindlessly from flower to flower, seemingly oblivious to the fact that they are almost a continent away from the land where they were hatched. Then one morning, as if on some heavenly cue, swarms of the beautiful creatures take wing and fly non-stop thousands of miles across mountain and sea to the valley where their short lives began. Nothing can keep them from home.

We are like that. The homing instinct grows within us as our days increase, until finally we are like the Christian lady whose story I began with. We want to go home.

A Healthy Hope

Right here we need to be clear. I do not belong to the Hemlock Society. I am not writing these words in praise of suicide. I write as one who loves life. I believe the Scripture that says God gave humans dominion over the earth and put us here to fill it and subdue it. With all the zest my soul can muster I am doing my part toward making a good earth better, and I intend do so as long as I draw breath. *Wanting to go home is not a death wish.* It is not a neurotic, Freudian desire to take the wimp's way out instead of facing life's harder moments with fortitude and faith.

Just as the members of a close family get excited when they anticipate holiday reunions with the people they love best, so all of us in God's family dream of the grand reunion when he calls us home.

The Old Testament uses an intriguing phrase to describe the deaths of Abraham and Isaac and Jacob and Aaron and Moses. Each of these great men, the Bible tells us, was "gathered to his people." Genesis 25:8 says, for example, that "Abraham breathed his last and died at a good old age, an old man and full of years; and he was gathered to his people."

I have sent some dear people ahead of me to heaven. No doubt you have, too. The prospect of dying becomes less foreboding when it is tempered with the awareness of who waits for us on the other side.

"Man goes to his eternal home," the Bible says. Instead of protesting with the unbelieving world, "How horrible!" God's people respond to this prospect by shouting, "Hallelujah!"

Home at Last

All who have read the Narnian Chronicles by C.S. Lewis have been indelibly touched by the picture he paints at the end of the final book, *The Last Battle*.

The children in the Narnia stories and all the delightful animal characters with them are aghast and saddened as they see the marvelous world of Narnia collapsing and dissolving, never to be again. The magical realm they have lived in and loved so dearly is dying.

But their dismay turns to delight, their anguish to amazement, as they discover that the new world they have just been ushered into is Narnia over again, but infinitely better. (A "new heaven" and a "new earth"?) All the old landmarks look the same, but the new Narnia is "a deeper country: every rock and flower and blade of grass looked as if it meant more."

The Unicorn in the story sums up the experience. "I have come home at last!" he exults. "This is my real country! I belong here. This is the land I have been looking for all my life, though I never knew it till now."

One day all who love the Lord will go home to the country where we really belong, to the place we have been looking for and getting ready for all of our lives. Then we'll be home.

Sheer Hope

We're never in deeper trouble than when we've lost hope.

A marriage may be shaken by tears and tantrums and tensions of all sorts, but it holds together until one of the mates loses hope. "Most of the divorced people I work with can tell me the exact day when they knew their marriage was over," one counselor told me. "The divorce may not have been filed for several months or even years after that day, but on that day they gave up all hope that the marriage could ever work."

I have seen a few churches that lost hope. It's enough to tear out your heart to see decent, lovable men and women plod woodenly through the motions of religion without even a flicker of hope that their work and worship will accomplish one blessed thing for God. A body this dead is fit for one of two things:

burial or resurrection! Without one or the other it soon stinks too much to keep around.

Hope is the vital ingredient of all corporate life forms: marriages, churches, companies, ball teams, armies, nations. None of these entities can survive long without hope.

But hope is most essential in our own hearts. We can weather almost any life trauma as long as we can see a suitable end to the ordeal. Take away all hope, however, and our hurting becomes unbearable.

God calls us at such low times to a special kind of faith. Defying all the data at hand, old Abraham believed in the Lord's ability to bless him and his aged wife with a child. "Against all hope," the Bible tells us, "Abraham in hope believed."

My colleague Dan Anders calls this "sheer hope." When all the facts are clearly against us and we still hang in there with the assurance that whatever God does in our life will be right, that is "sheer hope." It's the kind of hope Jesus demonstrated when he dreamed of the salvation of the world while his life ran red down the shaft of the cross, hope based not on physical circumstances but on faith in the One who holds our lives in his hands.

Real Estate in Anathoth

Let us fix our eyes on Jesus, the author and perfecter of our faith, who for the joy set before him endured the cross, scorning its shame, and sat down at the right hand of the throne of God. Consider him who endured such opposition from sinful men, so that you will not grow weary and lose heart (Hebrews 12:2-3).

Let me take you back in the Old Testament to a dismal time when hope had almost vanished in the land and the last sparks of faith were but a feeble flicker. Into this dark time God sent his servant Jeremiah, tagging him with what had to be the sorriest preaching assignment of all time.

Let's look in on Jeremiah on the morning described in Jeremiah 32, when his cousin Hanamel plans to drop by to see him. It's not the best day in Jeremiah's life. He's in jail. For what he's been preaching.

"Jerusalem is doomed," he's been telling everybody he sees. "That army camped outside the gates will make

it inside. Soon. The ditches they've been digging, the
dirt they've been piling up against the city walls — all
that work is just about complete. Any day now the
armies of Babylon will make their move and we'll be
powerless to stop them. At least, that's what God is
telling me. He says nothing we can do will stop the
enemy. Zedekiah may be king today, but in no time he'll
be a captive. He's about to get an all-expenses-paid trip
to central Iraq for a nose-to-nose visit with Babylon's
king, and he won't be coming home."

Well, you can imagine that King Zedekiah doesn't
have a whole lot of patience with that kind of preaching
on the palace steps. With an enemy as fierce as Babylon
camped outside his city's gates, he has enough trouble
without this harebrained preacher spooking the taxpay-
ers and intimidating the army. Not to mention that it
scares the king spitless to hear a God he barely believes
in predicting his imminent downfall. I'm afraid
Zedekiah is a lot like some folks I know today. He has
just enough faith to scare him and not enough to
comfort his soul. So Jeremiah's public predictions of
Zekediah's doom shake the faithless king to his roots.
"Arrest that nut!" the king orders his palace guard.
"Lock him up in the courtyard where he can't spread
his message of gloom and doom across the city." That's
where you and I find him. Not in a prison cell or a
dungeon, but still the prisoner of a very unhappy king.

As if Jeremiah doesn't have enough problems today,
God tips him off that he's about to get a visit from his
no-good cousin Hanamel. A few months ago, before the
battalions of Babylon swept through the countryside
north of Jerusalem, Hanamel farmed and ranched in the
fertile tribal lands of Benjamin. Along with the other

Benjaminites who were lucky enough to escape when the plundering hordes of Babylon raided their county, Hanamel is now hunkered down inside the walls of fortified Jerusalem, hiding on the last inch of Judean real estate not controlled by Nebuchadnezzar's warriors. Hanamel knows Jeremiah is right in what he preaches. He watched the defenses of Benjamin crumble before Babylon like Tinkertoys® squashed by a steamroller. This puny Judean army in Jerusalem won't fare any better. Their days are numbered. But with no real future in sight, Hanamel evidently figures he might as well make today count for something, so he's coming to see Cousin Jeremiah. To use the language of a con artist, Jeremiah is Hanamel's "mark."

Have you noticed what strange changes often take place in people when they lose their future? Something seems to go haywire inside folks when they stop expecting tomorrow.

It happens to young soldiers shipping out to a battlefront they may not come home from. Whether they're headed to Normandy or Iwo Jima or Seoul or Saigon, young men who expect to die often do crazy things. Some of the teetotalers get drunk. Some of the tightwads go out and blow every dollar they possess. And not a few of them rush out to marry girls they probably wouldn't even have dated before the war began.

Those of us who watched the collapse of traditional morality in the '60s know firsthand what happens to a generation that loses all hope of tomorrow. Convince them that an inevitable nuclear holocaust will soon end their days, and young people who might have grown up to be doctors or teachers or engineers become flower children instead. The NOW generation replaces religion with LSD and free love. They replace their parents with the gurus of hippie communes or Satanic cults. And they replace the tomorrow they have despaired of ever seeing with mindless orgies in the present moment.

Without hope to trim our sails, we drift aimlessly on the sea of life with no harbor in sight.

Without hope to illuminate our paths, we stumble like blind mice in an endless maze.

Without hope to kindle our dreams, we grow too soon old, and tired, and cynical, and depressed.

I wonder. Could this be why Romans 8:24 says we are saved "in hope"? We surely are in a mess without it.

This may be what we're seeing in Jeremiah's Jerusalem. When tomorrow evaporates, our ethics tend to evaporate. When hope dies for a church, or a nation, or a city, our moral moorings come untied. And the Hanamels among us, who may be fairly decent guys in normal times, lose touch with the day-to-day rules of honesty and decency and integrity.

If you've ever had a brother-in-law come to see you with a red-hot deal he expects you to finance, then you've got a pretty good idea of the feeling Jeremiah got in the pit of his stomach when God warned him that Cousin Hanamel would be stopping by today. Worse than that, God instructed Jeremiah to let Hanamel swindle him. Hanamel won't be selling swamp land in Louisiana, but the real estate bargain he's coming to offer Jeremiah is not much better. Hanamel is trying to unload the family farm on his cousin. Tucked up in the rolling hills near the village of Anathoth in the heart of Benjamin, it was a fine enough farm in the decades just past, but today nobody in his right mind would invest a penny on it. The whole Babylonian army is bivouacked not a stone's throw away. They've stolen all the grain, killed all the cows, burned the barns, and slaughtered all the Jewish neighbors who waited too late to evacuate. For days now the *Jerusalem Gazette* has been filled with tales of woe drifting in from the north part of the trade area. There won't be any trading going on there for a long time. At least not unless you speak fluent Babylonian.

You get the point, I'm sure. No sane Jew would buy a square foot of land near Anathoth today. But what does Hanamel have to lose? He's always heard that Jeremiah isn't quite right, so he decides to try him on for size. "Because you're family, Cousin Jeremiah," Hanamel oozes as he smiles like an Edsel salesman. "Because of our blood ties, I want to give you the first chance to own our family's fine acreage. Remember how green the grass is in the eastern meadow? And that stone well up there in the north forty. Do you remember how fresh and cool that water used to taste, Jeremiah, when you and I went rabbit-snaring up there along Ebenezer's fence line? Well, Cousin, I want you to own that well. I want you to have that meadow. Just put your shekels on the table and sign right here. Yessiree, have I got a deal for you today!"

Hanamel can't believe his eyes. This Jeremiah's a bigger goofball than the kinfolks said he was. With his gnarled thumb and his bony forefinger Jeremiah slowly extracts a well-worn pouch from the sash belt just below his left rib cage. Onto the tiny table in the corner of the palace courtyard the prophet shakes 17 silver coins. Six months ago Hanamel wouldn't have parted with his father's farm for ten times as much. Today he's getting ten times what it's worth. With a smile of disdain for his obviously obtuse cousin, Hanamel scoops up the shekels and hands Jeremiah the deed to a piece of land no Jew will break with a plow for almost a hundred years.

Do you know what's happening here? Do you see why God wants Jeremiah to buy into such a sucker deal? God wants this deed recorded publicly. He wants the city fathers to sign off as witnesses to the transaction. He wants everybody in town to know that Jeremiah is buying Hanamel's worthless farm. Why? Because in these dismal days when hope is in short supply God wants his people to start planning again for tomorrow. He wants to give them back their future. So he has Jeremiah tell everybody within earshot, "One day God will bring us back to this good land. And I'm getting ready for that day. Ready for the day when God's wrath finally has run out. When our punishment in Babylon is complete. In the time when God brings his people back to this place, my heirs will claim the farm I bought from Hanamel today. They will harvest its fruits and then they will know — all of you will know — that my faith in God and my hope for tomorrow are not just empty dreams. They are for real."

✹ ✹ ✹ ✹ ✹

"Faith is the substance of things hoped for," the old King James tells us. It is "the evidence of things not seen." In my early teen years when I first attempted the arduous task of writing an intelligible sermon outline, I used to come back to this text over and over. For some reason it intrigued me. At least in part because I loved all the Old Testament stories that are catalogued in the verses that follow immediately in that great 11th Chapter of Hebrews. But I must confess to you that no matter how long I pondered this famous verse, I did not understand it. I hadn't lived long enough to understand it. Because the preciousness and power of hope can be perceived only by a person who has been without it.

"The substance of things hoped for." What does that mean? The newer versions help a little to clarify this complex thought. The New International Version says, "Faith is being sure of what we hope for and certain of what we do not see." Faith, according to the Living Bible, "is the certainty that what we hope for is waiting for us, even though we cannot see it up ahead." That's the kind of faith Jeremiah has. He knows he won't be alive when the next generation comes back from Babylon to Anathoth to claim this farm he's just bought, but he's absolutely sure that they will come back. Because of his faith in God's promise, his hope is sure. He won't survive to see his hopes materialize, but he doesn't have to. If God says it will be, it will be.

Do you see the connection between faith and hope? This soul-stabilizing certainty that the promises of God will come true belongs only to people who know their Lord and trust in him without reservation. That's what Hebrews 11:1 is telling us. That faith and hope are inextricably linked together. Jeremiah's Jerusalem is filled with people who have lost hope because they have lost their God. They didn't think they needed him. When the stock market was high and the military was strong and the Babylonian army was looking the other direction for somebody to pick on, faith seemed to the playboys in Jerusalem to be an unnecessary nuisance. It just got in the way of their fun. After all, who needs God when they're healthy and wealthy and having a ball? But that's over now. With their enemy camped on their front doorstep and their God in a trash can, Jeremiah's neighbors are in a real mess. Where can they turn? Little did they know that when they scrapped their faith, they also discarded the possibility of hope. Now they wait helplessly as darkness engulfs them, and, having no faith, they have nowhere to turn to find light.

✳ ✳ ✳ ✳ ✳

Several chapters later Jeremiah tells us he got up one morning and headed north to inspect the property he had purchased from Hanamel. Unexpectedly the Babylonian army had backed off a bit from Jerusalem because of a temporary Egyptian threat, so Jeremiah thought he ought to take advantage of the first chance he'd had to check out his new farm. But he never made it. When he reached the gate on the Benjamin side of town, the police captain recognized him.

"I know what you're up to!" the officer accused Jeremiah. "You're deserting! You're heading out to cook up a plot with the Babylonians!" Buying that farm up in Anathoth had been what Eugene Peterson called "a deliberate act of hope," something a man without hope couldn't begin to fathom. The only explanation the gate guard could imagine was that Jeremiah had a card up his sleeve, that he had some sort of unsavory scheme in the works, and that he was using this trip to the Anathoth farm as a cover up. "All acts of hope expose themselves to ridicule," Eugene Peterson suggests, "because they seem impractical, failing to conform to visible reality." Only a believer could understand what

Jeremiah was doing that day. What began that morning as an innocent stroll in the country turned into a Rodney King nightmare. The officer arrested Jeremiah on the spot and summoned a gang of the prophet's worst political enemies, who had the hapless preacher flogged and then thrown into a jail controlled by one of the worst goons in the government.

"These accusations are totally false," Jeremiah assured the no-good king, "and you know they'll kill me in that jail."

King Zedekiah wavered briefly. "Get Jeremiah out of the dungeon," he ordered, "but don't let him out of the courtyard." Well, that was some improvement, but it didn't last long. When Jeremiah's captors heard what the king had done, these hotheaded, hateful young princes stormed into the palace demanding that Jeremiah be silenced. "Take him," the spineless king told them. "He's yours. Do whatever you want to." They did. By nightfall Jeremiah was sinking ever so slowly into the muddy bottom of the palace cistern, where these scoundrels had lowered him and left him to die.

Faith and hope are stained-glass words. They sound pretty, don't they? Especially when they are coupled with love in 1 Corinthians 13. But if we want to see real hope and real faith, we need to slide down into that well alongside Jeremiah. We need to get plastered with the muck and mire of that makeshift dungeon. We need to feel the hate, the hostility, of the enemies of God who put him there. We need to taste the nearness of death, the fate we've been consigned to because we dare to speak truthfully for God. Then, maybe with Jeremiah's help, we can glimpse the stern reality of the true nature of faith and hope.

Faith and hope are the only explanation for the courage of a man like Romanian pastor Laszlo Tokes. Despite life-threatening imprisonments and beatings by the Communist tyrants who controlled his country, this Christian minister continued faithfully to lead and teach the village church where the authorities had exiled him to remove his influence from his city parish. That Christmas, when state police again were arresting dissidents and violence was breaking out across Romania, Tokes was afraid for his own life. He knew they might come for him. But he sat down behind bolted doors to read again the stories of our Lord's birth as told by Matthew and Luke. He would preach a Christmas sermon if they let him, but it would focus not on angels or shepherds or wisemen or mangers. He knew that the Christmas Scripture which would speak most plainly to his oppressed people would be Matthew's stark description of Herod's massacre of the babies in Bethlehem. Romanian Christians knew only too well this kind of mistreatment by a hostile ruler. On Christmas morning, however, church bells rang and Christians across Romania rejoiced because of the glorious news that the Communist dictator Ceauşescu had been arrested and the long tyranny of Communist rule had been broken. The dogged faith and hope of those oppressed Christians were rewarded when, for the first time in 40 years, they celebrated Christmas as a public holiday.

Do you want to see faith and hope at work? Then look at our Lord Jesus, the writer of Hebrews bids us, "who for the joy set before him" — because of what he hoped for — "endured the cross, scorning its shame, and sat down at the right hand of the throne of God."

Then the Hebrews writer pleads with us, "Consider him who endured such opposition from sinful men." May his example of faith and hope inspire in us an unwavering determination to stand strong in the face of every test as we trust in him.

The Walking Dead

The earth shook and the rocks split. The tombs broke open and the bodies of many holy people who had died were raised to life. They came out of the tombs, and after Jesus' resurrection they went into the holy city and appeared to many people (Matthew 27:51b-52).

This is a curious verse that raises more questions than it answers. I grant you that most of the questions are speculative and unanswerable, but I still wonder about them.

1) The text says "many holy people" were raised. How many is "many"? Were families all over Jerusalem startled to see dead relatives knocking on their doors?

2) How long did these resurrected people stay around this time? Were they allowed only a one-day visit among the living, sort of like the hero in *Carousel*? If they were given several months or years of resurrected life, why don't the Scriptures tell us about such people

in the early church? Surely they would have been notable by their very presence. Can you imagine a sermon by a Christian convert who had come back from Hades after lengthy visits with Abraham and Moses and Elijah? He could tell you what Moses really meant when he wrote Exodus 34:26. He'd be handy to have around.

3) If a fellow died of cancer or heart trouble or diabetes, did his resurrected body still suffer from these maladies? Did his resurrection on Good Friday awaken him to the same pains he died with? That would be horrible, wouldn't it? If the dead person was an amputee, did he emerge from his tomb with both feet again intact? Our Lord's resurrection body was human (he ate and was touchable, according to the Gospels), but he also floated through walls. Did his comrades-in-new-life that Easter morning enjoy the same sort of bodies? Just wondering.

4) The text says the tombs burst open during the earthquake that shook Judea when Jesus died, but these resurrected men and women did not enter Jerusalem until Easter morning when Jesus arose. What were they doing from Friday until Sunday morning? Did they lie dead in the open sepulchers, awaiting the life-giving Spirit to work His magic on Jesus and them together? Or did they wake up Friday and accompany Jesus on his preaching mission to "the spirits in prison"?

5) Were the folks in Jerusalem happy to see their departed relatives reappearing? Think about it. How do you suppose the son felt when his mother returned to find out that he had cheated his brothers and sisters out of their share of the family inheritance? Was he glad to

see Mama? If, after his wife's departure, a man had married a woman his previous wife could not stand, how thrilled would this couple be to see Wife #1 coming in the door? I can imagine all manner of inconveniences in having the dead suddenly reappear. Can't you? But I can also imagine the jubilation of parents who recovered a son lost in war or a daughter taken by leukemia. Don't you know those families had a grand homecoming?

6) The text tells us that those who came out of the tombs that Sunday morning were "holy" people. Does that mean the Spirit refused to resurrect liars and thieves and drunkards and racists? If so, how many of us would have been eligible for resurrection that day? When you think about it, it makes sense to leave the evil people in their graves. Who would want the town to be overrun with revived rapists and robbers and rascals of every sort? When we execute criminals, we intend for them to stay dead, don't we?

7) Don't you know the people in town were shocked when all these long-dead people showed up? I can just imagine the scene at the synagogue when their former rabbi shows up unexpectedly.

"Levi, I just fired the synagogue custodian."
"Why'd you do a thing like that, Saul?"
"Because he'd been drinking on the Sabbath!"
"Saul, all Jews drink on the Sabbath. . ."
"Yeah, I know that, Levi, but this was different. He was drunk. So drunk that he was still hallucinating on Sunday morning."
"Really?"
"You better believe it. He told me this wild tale about seeing Rabbi Zadok walking around the synagogue this morning. Said the old man was shaking his head and muttering his disapproval of the

modern-art menorah we installed on the wall beside the pulpit. He said old Zadok threw a fit when he found our bowling team plaques on the wall where he used to put stars on our charts for memorizing verses from the Torah. Levi, it was kinda creepy hearing the custodian talk like he did. I think he really believed he had seen Zadok, and you and I both know the rabbi's been dead for 18 years."

"Saul, I don't know how to tell you this, but I saw him, too. And so did Mary and Simeon and Eleazar. I thought I was cracking up at first, Saul, but old Zadok smiled and told me not to doubt the power and goodness of God. 'After all,' he said, 'haven't we Pharisees been insisting on the reality of the resurrection for the past three centuries? Why should it surprise us when what we've been preaching turns out to be true?' I thought he made a good point, Saul."

"Have you been drinking, too, Levi? Are you telling me the truth? If dear old Zadok's here, I want to see him, too. Let's go find him. . ."

Well, you can see that I had some fun chasing the questions Matthew stirred up in my head when he told me the tombs were opened and the dead came to town. I just wish he had told us more about it.

As I tossed these questions around in my brain, however, it occurred to me that the sort of questions this Scripture provokes are exactly the kind of things most of us wonder about when we contemplate our own resurrection, aren't they?

When I'm resurrected, what will I be like? people want to know.
- ❖ Will I be pretty? (Even if I'm not now.)
- ❖ Will I be healthy? (Despite my present ailments.)
- ❖ Will I be young, or old, or weak, or strong?
- ❖ If I'm eaten by a lion, as the poet John Donne surmised,

and he scatters me in his stools across the plains, will God be able to reassemble my processed atoms on resurrection day?

❖ If I drown in the ocean and the fish duplicate the lion's role at forty fathoms, will I miss that glorious day when God opens the graves to call us heavenward?

❖ When I'm resurrected, how much will I remember about earth's sorrows? (God promises there will be no tears in his heaven.)

❖ Will I be married? (Jesus says No.)

❖ Will I be male or female? (Jesus says Neither.)

❖ Will I know my loved ones? (All the scriptural evidence says Yes.)

❖ Will I still be me? (Without doubt, and if you've been living for Jesus, you'll be glad you're you!)

We have so many questions about our own resurrection, don't we? Listen as the Lord answers some them.

In Dr. Eugene Peterson's superb new free translation *The Message*, 1 Corinthians 15:35-58 tells us this:

> *Some skeptic is sure to ask, "Show me how resurrection works. Give me a diagram; draw me a picture. What does this 'resurrection body' look like?" If you look at this question closely, you realize how absurd it is. There are no diagrams for this kind of thing. We do have a parallel experience in gardening. You plant a "dead" seed; soon there is a flourishing plant. There is no visual likeness between seed and plant. You could never guess what a tomato would look like by looking at a tomato seed. What we plant in the soil and what grows out of it don't look anything alike. The dead body that we bury in the ground and the resurrection body that comes from it will be dramatically different.*

You will notice that the variety of bodies is stunning. Just as there are different kinds of seeds, there are different kinds of bodies — humans, animals, birds, fish — each unprecedented in its form. You get a hint at the diversity of resurrection glory by looking at the diversity of bodies not only on earth but in the skies — sun, moon stars — all these varieties of beauty and brightness. And we're only looking at pre-resurrection "seeds" — who can imagine what the resurrection "plants" will be like!

This image of planting a dead seed and raising a live plant is a mere sketch at best, but perhaps it will help in approaching the mystery of the resurrection body — but only if you keep in mind that when we're raised, we're raised for good, alive forever! The corpse that's planted is no beauty, but when it's raised, it's glorious. Put in the ground weak, it comes up powerful. The seed sown is natural; the seed grown is supernatural — same seed, same body, but what a difference from when it goes down in physical mortality to when it is raised up in spiritual immortality!

We follow this sequence in Scripture: The First Adam received life, the Last Adam is a life-giving Spirit. Physical life comes first, then spiritual — a firm base shaped from the earth, a final completion coming out of heaven. The First Man was made out of earth, and people since then are earthy; the Second Man was made out of heaven, and people now can be heavenly. In the same way that we've worked from our earthy origins, let's embrace our heavenly ends.

I need to emphasize, friends, that our natural, earthy lives don't in themselves lead us by their very nature into the kingdom of God. Their very "nature" is to die, so how could they "naturally" end up in the Life kingdom?

But let me tell you something wonderful, a mystery I'll probably never fully understand. We're not all going to die — but we are all going to be changed. You hear a blast to end all blasts from a trumpet, and in the time

*that you look up and blink your eyes — it's over. On
signal from that trumpet from heaven, the dead will be
up and out of their graves, beyond the reach of death,
never to die again. At the same moment and in the same
way, we'll all be changed. In the resurrection scheme of
things, this has to happen: everything perishable taken
off the shelves and replaced by the imperishable, this
mortal replaced by the immortal. Then the saying will
come true:*

  "Death swallowed by triumphant Life!
  Who got the last word, oh, Death?
  Oh, Death, who's afraid of you now?"

*It was sin that made death so frightening and law-code
guilt that gave sin its leverage, its destructive power.
But now in a single victorious stroke of Life, all three —
sin, guilt, death — are gone, the gift of our Master,
Jesus Christ. Thank God!*

  *With all this going for us, my dear, dear friends, stand
your ground. And don't hold back. Throw yourselves
into the work of the Master, confident that nothing you
do for him is a waste of time or effort.*

Or, consider the simpler answer in 1 John 3:2:

*Dear friends, now we are children of God, and what we
will be has not yet been made known. But we know that
when he appears, we shall be like him. . . .*

That's all I need to know.

The Last of Life

The length of our days is seventy years — or eighty, if we have the strength; yet their span is but trouble and sorrow, for they quickly pass, and we fly away. Teach us to number our days aright, that we may gain a heart of wisdom. (Psalm 90:10,12).

"Pastor Shelburne?" I didn't recognize my caller's voice, but the pastor in me switched on instantly. Not because she used the word. It was something in her voice that raised all the flags, pushed all the buttons, triggering responses ingrained by almost four decades of ministry. Unconsciously my brain catalogued what I knew at once about this woman I had never met.

Not one of "ours," I smiled. She doesn't use our vocabulary or know our shibboleths.

Probably in her 70s, I thought, without really thinking.

And troubled, I instantly surmised, before she spoke another word. Something about the way she spoke my name revealed an urgency. Almost a desperation. So I dropped what I was doing and gave her my full attention. "Pastor Shelburne?" she had begun.

"Speaking," I identified myself.

"Oh, really?" She seemed flustered. "I didn't dream I'd be talking to you. Are you really Pastor Shelburne?"

"Yes," I assured her. "Is there some way I can help you?"

"Well, I've been seeing the ads about your book, and they brought you to my mind. I thought maybe. . ." The sentence trailed off into an awkward silence.

Is she crying? I wondered. *Or maybe trying to get up courage to talk about something she's ashamed of?*

"Do you counsel with people who don't attend your congregation?" she finally asked.

"I used to do a lot of that," I told her, "but my calendar is too full these days for me to find time to attempt much of it anymore."

"Well, I think you're the only person who can help me. I really need to visit with you," she pressed.

Why me? I thought. *What has made her single me out as a source of counsel or comfort?*

So I asked her, "Can you give me an idea of the nature of your troubles?"

"It's too complicated to explain on the telephone," she replied. And then she launched into a rambling answer punctuated repeatedly with agonizing pauses and lapses of coherence. "My troubles go back a lot of years," she began, and then moaned, "Oh! I can't tell you how bad I've been hurt!"

Tears momentarily muffled her voice, but she quickly stuffed them and announced emphatically, "It's all coming together! Finally I think I know why it's all been happening! I just need to talk with you and let you see that I've figured out what's been going on. Don't you think I ought to share it with somebody so they'll know, just in case I die or something?"

Variations of this nebulous explanation took up at least the next five minutes of our conversation. The harder she tried to explain her agitation, the muddier she made matters and the more agitated she became. Somewhere in it all I did discover that she had heard me preach. At a Lenten service last spring at a nearby Presbyterian church. She also read my newspaper column every Saturday morning, so she felt like she knew me. And I was the only minister she did know, at least in our town. It was obvious she needed to talk to somebody, so, despite a calendar already bulging beyond any possibility, I agreed to see her.

Within limits. "I will clear 45 minutes this afternoon for a single session," I told her, "but I am not able to offer you ongoing, long-term counseling. If your problems are severe, maybe I can assist you in finding someone else to help you in the days ahead." And then, for the first time in a 15-minute call, I asked for her name.

She hesitated. Until now the comfort of anonymity had freed her tongue. Now, with her name on the line, she was unsure. After a brief pause, though, she took the plunge. She *would* seek help in dealing with her problems (whatever they were). She *would* schedule a place on my calendar. So she told me, "My name is Misty Meadows." And she spelled it for me, just to be sure I understood.

"Can you come at 2:00 this afternoon?" I asked her.

"Oh," she gasped. "I don't know if I could possibly get it all sorted out so soon. After all. . ." Her voice trailed off into some never-never land of her thoughts, and then she rejoined me, "I've got to try to explain it all to you. And I just don't know if I can." Again she paused, mumbling to herself. "But," she resumed with a tone of desperation, "I've just *got* to make it clear to you. You've got to help me know what to do."

Finally we settled on two o'clock. Doubting that her confused mind could grasp them, I gave her detailed instructions for finding our lost-in-the-neighborhood church building, and then I hung up the phone, wondering what in the world had vexed this poor woman so. In almost twenty minutes of conversation she never had been able to tell me.

✳ ✳ ✳ ✳ ✳

Face-to-face that afternoon, I found out why.

Misty Meadows hobbled the few feet from her maroon Nissan to my study door, steadied by an elegant cane. That walking stick, and the aging fashion-designer suit she wore, were vestiges of better times when money had been abundant. Of a time when she entered offices like mine with a flair. Subtle hints of former dignity kept signalling me that this poor confused soul in the chair opposite my desk had not too long ago been a lady with poise and panache, most of which was sadly missing that day.

The 45 minutes I offered her stretched into twice that long, as I suspected it would. Not once in that time was she able to give me a clear, simple statement of what she saw as her problem. Instead, from her disjointed ramblings I gleaned scraps of data about unconnected epochs of her almost 80 years.

Some years ago she had buried one husband, whom she loved fiercely. But he had hurt her. Deeply. And often.

But he was a prince. A rich one, too. Who hurt her. Often. And deeply. But she loved him and always would. . . .

The next husband hurt her, too. Five and a half years later she dumped him. Walked away from that mistake. Never told her kids how shabbily he had treated her. Still didn't want them to know. But he was awful. . . .

But she would make their pastor pay. Which pastor? The one in Miami, Florida. Who else? The one who knew her first husband and kids when they were a family together at home. Didn't I think she ought to make that pastor publicly explain why he had hurt her so badly? By golly, she would. She had it all figured out now. Finally it was all making sense to her. She was going to Miami and make that pastor explain in public why he'd hurt her so much, why he kept on hurting her. Why did he treat her that way?

"What way?" I asked her. How was this pastor hurting her? My question drew only tears and agitation, but never a specific answer. Nor did she seem able to answer similar questions about her husbands and other unnamed personages of the past whom she also blamed for her present distress. She had it all figured out now, she assured me, but what "it" was, she couldn't tell me.

"What do you think I should do?" she pled. "Please tell me what to do."

"I'm sure I don't understand your whole situation, Mrs. Meadows," I replied with what had to be the understatement of the ages, "but I advise you not to do anything at all until you've talked this over with some family member you trust. Maybe your son in Ohio." More than once she had mentioned him in positive tones.

"Oh, I don't want to worry him with my affairs," she demurred.

"But, Mrs. Meadows, that's what sons are for," I pushed her. "Let them help you. If not the one in Ohio, then perhaps your younger boy in Arkansas. I'm sure either one of them would be willing to help you think this matter through before you do something as serious as you are suggesting." The truth is that I didn't know exactly what she might do, but some of her threats were ominous.

When my own mother died, she was about the age of Misty Meadows. About the same build, too. With swept-up hair the same shade of gray. And, before the malignant brain tumor did its number on her, with a lot of the same wit and pluck I suspect Misty Meadows possessed before her present distress unhinged her. I certainly would have appreciated it if a minister I had never met in a town I had never visited made sure that my mama consulted me before she had a chance to humiliate herself and maybe to wound innocent people who somehow had surfaced in a paranoid delusion that tormented her soul.

"Before you do anything, Mrs. Meadows," I urged her, "talk to your boys. At least, confide in one of them. Let them advise you." But I could tell, as she began gathering up her scarf and purse and gloves that this was not what she wanted me to tell her. I watched out my study window as she drove off the church parking lot. What would she do next? Would she catch a plane to Miami to beard the pastor she remembered so angrily? Would she go home to her condo and cry herself to sleep, perhaps to wake up feeling better? Would her doctor take her off the new blood-pressure medication he gave her last week, and by that simple measure free this sweet lady from her paranoid terrors and tears? As I watched her drive away, I said a prayer. And I called a mutual friend she'd mentioned. "She's very unhappy right now," I told him, "and very confused. Please check on her."

What would you have done?

✳ ✳ ✳ ✳ ✳

"Grow old with me," one poet coaxed a friend, and promised, "the best is yet to be." Did he tell the truth? Or should that poet have been indicted for fraud and false advertising?

"Gray hair is a crown of glory," the Scriptures proclaim. When I look at my own sainted father, now well past 80, I heartily agree. The gray hairs he has left bear mute testimony — every single one of them — to the vast wisdom he has accumulated through years of patient ministry to God's broken people and through decades of passionate study of God's holy word. My father gained his "crown" by faithfully enduring tribulations and attacks that would have destroyed a lesser man. He may be living proof of one fellow's homespun theory that the pigment in our hair drains out in our tears. Even when, as in my father's case, those tears are shed more privately and more sparingly than the tragedies of his life might have warranted.

Anyway, my father's gray hair certainly is "a crown of glory," as the ancient wiseman wrote. But that unknown writer failed to mention that glory is not the only thing a person gets along with gray hair. Arthritis and atherosclerosis and Alzheimer's might head the list, and that won't even get us past the A's. As our years increase, so do our losses. Too often old age tragically can be defined as a time of lost health, lost memory, lost

stamina, lost spouses, lost careers, lost friends, and —
for people like Misty Meadows — lost dignity.

For some, the adjustments these losses require are
devastating. Except for the rare George Burns types who
appear to be ageless and untiring, most octogenarians
find their physical strength waning. They have to pace
themselves. I remember when my father finally admitted that his 12-to-14-hour work days were no longer
realistic. That an afternoon nap was more than a luxury.

Almost as hard to accept as the physical restraints
are the social constrictions of advanced years. "By the
time you get to be our age, you've outlived most of
your friends," one 80-year-old man told me as we
talked about how many people might show up for his
wife's funeral. He was right. Most of those who
attended were associates of his kids and grandkids.

Can you imagine the trauma of losing the right to
drive? Or of losing the eyesight necessary to watch TV
or to read? Or of losing the ability to hear and, conse-
quently, the ability to share in daily chatter with friends
and family? In our fast-paced world, the loss of mobil-
ity seems to pain us most of all.

If we live long enough, though, most of us will get
there, won't we? Some of us are there already. Blessed
are those who reach their final decades surrounded by
loving friends and families who offset the deficits of
aging by doing for us what we can no longer do for
ourselves. Nobody is lonelier than an old person alone.

Few Choices

I can't count the times when someone commented,
as we were discussing the sad plight of some elderly
friend, "I don't ever want to grow old and get in that

condition." Who does? But we don't get too many choices do we? Since most of us would rule out euthanasia or suicide as a Christian choice, we are left then to accept whatever comes our way. Sometimes it's not good.

My mother's father came from a family where folks lasted a long time. He had every hope of living well into his 90s, or beyond, probably in good shape most of the way. But a defective pin in the steering mechanism of his old Ford pickup changed all that. In his robust early 70s, stronger than most men half his age, my grandfather survived the wreck that day, but the steering wheel crushed his rib cage and left him a frail, hurting, dependent old man. Now unable to check on his sheep three times a day, as he always had done, or to care for his livestock, hardly able, in fact, to walk from one room of his tiny house to another, my grandfather's last years were not good ones. Through no fault of his own. He had no choice in the matter.

Lots of us won't. The maladies that steal our strength, the frailties that divest us of dignity will come upon us, as they do for so many, in spite of anything we do or don't do. Thankfully, God will soften these humiliating days for some of us by allowing our minds to fail before our bodies, so that we'll be largely unaware of the distress of those days. Then our kids and others we leave behind will bear the pain, but we won't know enough to care. Even that fate will not likely be an option we get to choose. Every day of our lives we are clay in the hands of the heavenly Potter, and he shapes each moment as part of his eternal plan. Our sense of being in control when we're young and strong and virile is largely an illusion — an illusion that fades in our last years, when increasingly we are not in control of anything.

Choices We Do Make

We have painted a false picture, however, unless we admit that some of our choices do determine the quality of our twilight years. One sweet lady, looking back at her high school annual and reading the comments of her classmates, was surprised at how many of them commented on her bright smile. Realizing that she had allowed herself over the years to become too often angry and too often critical, she admitted, "I don't smile as much these days." And she resolved to change that. This decision will change the quality of her years four decades from now. "Grumpy Old Men" is not just the title of a movie. And, unfortunately, the adjectives aren't reserved just for men.

A lady who managed a chain of nursing homes talked to me several years ago. She was an expert in aging, having closely observed hosts of elderly clients through the years. She had a theory. "When we grow old and lose most of our conscious control," she said, "then the person we really are tends to come out. When we are still 'at ourselves,' we stifle our anger. We don't say the ugly words we think, or express the feelings that boil inside us. But when our minds fail and our inhibitions melt away, then the real person we kept bottled up all those years comes out, and meek little ladies sometimes begin to swear like sailors." Let me hasten to qualify that she was not describing people with a disease like Alzheimer's, where anger seems to be generated by chemical or neural impairment.

If this gerontologist was right, then the wisdom of

the Scriptures appears even wiser, when they advise us in our strong young days to focus our hearts and minds on things that will bless us and those around us in the days to come. "Whatever is true, whatever is noble, whatever is right, whatever is pure, whatever is lovely, whatever is admirable — if anything is excellent or praiseworthy — think about such things." You don't have to be an expert to know that if we learn when we're 30 or 40 to be gracious and tender and forgiving, we're far more likely to be sweet-tempered and sociable when we're 80 or 90. And that's a choice we make. Every day.

Do I dare to mention lifestyle and diet choices younger folks make, choices that are almost certain to affect the quality of later years? When I stand beside the bedside of an emphysema patient gasping for his last breaths before death, I wonder how many of my smoking friends would opt for such an end. One of my most brilliant friends today is reduced to an almost totally dependent cripple because of years of uncontrolled calorie consumption. His life probably will be several decades shorter than his father's, and his last years will be painful and dismal because of poor choices he made in his prime.

If you want to avoid some of the agony and anguish of old age, live smart and make good choices early in life.

Learning To Depend

I also have a theory about old age. One I can't prove. But I'll share it with you anyway. We come into this world totally helpless, don't we? All of us. Somebody else has to feed us and carry us and bathe us and clothe us. We spend our first years learning to trust our parents, learning to depend on our fellow human beings and our God. Here's my theory. Could it be that God uses our final years on earth to renew this lesson of dependence? Once more we are likely to find ourselves increasingly helpless. And most of us don't like it. We want to be independent. We want to handle this job all by ourselves. But the time comes when somebody else drives for us. Somebody else cooks for us. Somebody else attends even to our simplest bodily needs and functions. And we leave this world, shorn of any pretense of strength or dignity. Once more we are totally dependent. Just as the heavenly Father means for all his children to be all along.

Have you heard the promise in Isaiah 46:3-4? Here are words designed to get you through the darkest days of later life. "Listen to me," God assures us, "you whom I have upheld since you were conceived, and have carried since your birth. Even to your old age and gray hairs I am he, I am he who will sustain you. I have made you and I will carry you; I will sustain you and I will rescue you."

God Is Up to Something

After they had been severely flogged, they were thrown into prison. . ..
About midnight Paul and Silas were praying and singing hymns to God,
and the other prisoners were listening (Acts 16:23, 25).

It's hard to tell when God is up to something, isn't it?

Reading the Bible as we do, with centuries of hindsight to let us know what God had in mind at a particularly difficult moment, we may fail to realize that fellows like Paul and Silas didn't have that advantage.

Every time I read chapter 16 of Acts, I come away amazed at the way Paul and Silas reacted to the abuse they suffered in Philippi that night. Beaten within an inch of their lives, bloodied and brutalized by the sadistic Roman whips, locked in stocks in the deepest dungeon at the jailer's disposal, the preachers had to be in direst agony. Pain from the whip-cut gashes on their torsos must have burned like hellfire. The ache of bodies bludgeoned by bullies must have made even the slight movement an obscene nightmare.

"Why me?" I expect to hear Silas whine to God. "We've been out there working our tails off, Lord, covering the city for you. We've preached a jillion sermons. Baptized Lydia and everybody in her house. We even exorcised a demon this morning, Lord. And what do we get for it? You let this happen to us. How come, Lord? What did we do to deserve pain like this?"

That's what I expect to hear from the darkness of that dungeon. Because that's the sort of moaning I'd do if I were in their shoes.

I know my tolerance for abuse. When some upset saint peels the skin off my head like the angry lady I tried to minister to last week, I protest. I don't like to be abused and misused. Even in the name of Jesus. I confess to you that I have a long way to go before my faith makes me praise God for a dose of undeserved criticism.

I complain when the pulpit's a bit too warm. Or when the pews are hard and the service runs 20 minutes too long. That's my tolerance level for ministerial suffering.

But there in that jail sit Paul and Silas, wracked with excruciating pain as a result of a whipping they did nothing to deserve, and they respond by singing hymns and loudly praising God for considering them worthy to suffer like Jesus did. Christ got nails in his hands and stripes from the cat-o'-nine-tails across his back. Now, with their own stripes, Paul and Silas are just that much more like their Lord. So they rejoice! To me, that's incredible.

Of course, you and I know twenty centuries later that God planned to shake the jail apart that night. You and I know now that the jailer who supervised the preachers' torture that afternoon would be baptized by the same men before daybreak. You and I know that Paul's suffering in the jail that night resulted in the best church Paul planted in his entire ministry.

In the difficult days ahead it was this church in Philippi who took care of Paul, regardless. When he found himself in jail in distant cities (as he often did), somebody from Philippi always showed up with food and care. They knew he would go hungry unless somebody outside the prison provided. They always did.

When Paul found himself in areas where he could not ask locals to support his ministry financially, Philippi always stepped in with needed funds. "Time and again you sent help to me," Paul wrote to them years later. "Over and over you met my needs." And he was grateful.

But in the dungeon that night, soaked with the blood of the evening's flogging, Paul had no way to know that the persecutions he bore would be so fruitful. At that point he could not possibly have known what God was up to.

Not any more than you and I can when life turns suddenly sour, and sorrow engulfs our souls. Years later we may be able to look back and see God's hand, shaping, moving, leading for our good. But today's darkness makes it hard to see tomorrow's light.

That's why the reaction of Paul and Silas in the Philippian prison that night amazes me so. Even in the darkness, without a glimpse of God's future purpose, they trusted Him and sang his praises.

＊ ＊ ＊ ＊ ＊

Two thousand years and at least that many miles away from the jail God shook apart that night in Philippi, let me tell you another prison tale. One that is still unfolding even as I write it.

Lori and Eugene Nij serve the Lord today in San Raymundo, Guatemala. Not too many years ago Lori met Eugene at the Colegio Biblico, where he went to prepare for ministry not long after his conversion. Lori and Eugene fell in love and got married, both of them committed to the goal of returning soon to his home area of Guatemala to start a church. That church now exists, along with an orphanage. And now a Christian school has been started. That's the good news. But the story doesn't end there.

Although international headlines have largely ignored it, Guatemala presently is torn by civil strife, with warring factions struggling over issues too local and too complicated for most of us outsiders to fathom. Eugene (the Guatemalans call him Queno) and Lori knew when they began their work that they would have to contend not only with the political upheavals and hostilities that disrupt the country, but they also knew they were planting a Protestant work in a region that has been dominated by "old world" Catholicism for centuries. They expected opposition and got it. Local authorities did not welcome their ministry.

Couple this with another scenario that only a local Guatemalan can appreciate fully, and you'll be ready to understand the nightmare that has invaded the Nijs' lives. Rebels against the existing government have learned that they can finance their insurgency through kidnappings. Ransom payments can be lucrative, so kidnapping in this part of Guatemala has become epidemic.

On a recent morning in the San Raymundo town square, one such kidnapping was foiled by local merchants who responded to the hysterical screams of a young mother. Rushing to her aid, they caught two women who were trying to steal the mother's baby. Eugene (Queno) got involved obliquely when he tried to keep the kidnappers from being beaten to death on the spot. When police arrived to haul the kidnappers away, the Guatemalan preacher warned the officers that they needed to transport the kidnappers to jail in another town for their own protection. Having thus done all that he could do to prevent needless bloodshed, he returned to his office to finish his day's work, dismissing the kidnapping affair as a matter now beyond his concern.

Unknown to Queno, the police ignored his wise advice. That evening, when the men of the town came in from the fields, their distraught wives incited them to tear down the jail and kill the kidnappers. By the time police responded to the mayhem, one of the offending women had been killed and the other seriously injured. Queno's fears had come true.

Several days passed and the incident had faded from Queno's immediate focus when the police unexpectedly knocked on his front door with warrant in hand. Some angry soul in the bowels of the local constabulary had spotted the nebulous link between the preacher and the lynching and, acting on motivations known only to himself and those who join him in disliking the Nijs' ministry, this unknown official thug decided he had stumbled onto the perfect opportunity to snuff out Lori and Queno's work. So he had the preacher arrested. Although more than 300 witnesses, including the police officers who broke up the lynch mob, can testify that Queno was nowhere near the jail when the kidnapper was slain, the authorities have charged him with murder one and have thrown him into one of the area's toughest prisons, a place where survival is an every-minute concern for any inmate.

Within three days of Queno's arrest, e-mail flashes about this miscarriage of justice hit my computer from literally all over the globe. From Africa. From Houston. From upstate New York. From New Mexico. Pick on one missionary and they all rally to defend. That's how it ought to be for all Christians. Pick on one of us and you've got the rest of us to deal with. Queno has lots of friends today in places he never heard of. That's for sure.

The rest of the tale I draw, piecing together bits that have filtered in day by day from sources I can't always identify because the messages have been forwarded so many times on the Internet. I will borrow some of the words used in those reports, although I understand that the original author is Lori's brother, Dean Pinney, who lives in New Mexico. He didn't write it for credit, of course. He wrote to solicit prayers and support for Queno and Lori.

When Queno got to prison, the first report says, he found that he would be put in the general population, right in the same holding area occupied by murderers, rapists, and terrorists — the nastiest of the nasty. Most of the toughs in that federal prison have been convicted of capital crimes. They have been put there to die.

How could a gentle fellow like Queno survive in a hell-hole like that? When the prison doors clanged shut behind him, he fell instantly to his knees and began to pray. Within minutes, one report says, other inmates inched up to him and asked him to pray for them. As the crowd grew, he rose from prayer and began to preach. Soon the convicts around Queno, like the prison people Paul and Silas ministered to in Philippi, began to cry out, "What must we do to be saved?" For hours this unlikely scene continued. Even the guards drew near to listen.

That night Queno called Lori. Inmates in that prison are never allowed access to a telephone, but the guards who were touched by Queno's preaching spirited him into the head office and allowed the missionary a chance to talk to his frightened wife and to pray with her. Many of the earliest reports were passed in this way from inside the prison walls through Lori and, via e-mail, around the world.

On his first day in the prison, as Queno began to preach, a huge, menacing fellow approached him and introduced himself to the preacher as "the devil himself." From the way the other inmates reacted, it was obvious that this brute ran things in this horrid place.

"Stop preaching!" he warned Queno. "Now!"

"I perceive that you are a man who likes power," the preacher told him, and when the tough-guy grunted, Queno continued, "The power you think you've found in the Mafia, and the power you wield inside these walls is nothing compared to the power you could have." This surprising idea caught his antagonist's attention. "Real power is available in only one place — in Jesus Christ," Queno instructed his new student. At once he prayed with him and spent most of that night teaching the man about Jesus. The next day this massive man whose word was law in the prison yard, announced to the entire prison population, "Anybody who messes with the preacher messes with me!"

In central American prisons the inmates depend on friends and family outside the walls for any food they get. Knowing this, Lori began bringing to Queno the once-a-day meal allowed in this particular facility. But on the second day her trip to the prison was somehow prevented. When it became obvious to the other inmates that Queno would have nothing to eat that day, one by one they began to tear off and pass to the hungry preacher bits of their own bread. One inmate said, "You've fed us all day from the plate of God. Now let us feed you from our plates."

Who could possibly have planned what is happening today in that Guatemalan prison? Is there a mission society or a group of elders anywhere in the Kingdom wise enough to plot such a strategy for reaching that cluster of criminals with the Good News of Jesus? God is up to something in Guatemala, but he didn't bother to let Lori and Queno in on his plans for pulling it off.

For two weeks now at the time of this writing Queno's plight has made the front page of the national newspaper. At his first legal hearing, the judge tongue-lashed the District Attorney for bringing him a case in which he had no supporting evidence. Guatemalans know this, and the D.A.'s targeted victim is quickly becoming a national figure, who will undoubtedly draw massive crowds anywhere he preaches when God sees fit for him to be free again.* Meanwhile, Queno

---

*In an e-mail message received a week after I wrote this chapter, we learned that the judge is pressuring the prosecutor to resolve the charges against Queno, and even the president of Guatamala is being inundated with requests for justice, requests coming literally from all over the

continues to preach and pray all day inside the prison walls, bringing more converts to Jesus every day. And in San Raymundo, Lori reports, for five days there have been lines of people as far as the eyes can see, people lined up at the lawyer's office to give depositions. So far over a thousand people who knew Queno and were touched by his good ministry have testified to his blamelessness. And local observers say the line still doesn't look like it has moved, so many more are waiting to speak on his behalf.

Citizens of the San Raymundo region, men and women whose annual family income is equivalent to about a hundred dollars, are coming to Lori's house with money they had stored up to feed their own families. "Let us help you pay your legal bills," they tell her. "Let us help you feed your family while Queno is in jail."

As I mentioned earlier, Guatemala is a Catholic country, a place where the Nijs' Protestant ministry has often been unwelcome. But on the day Queno was arrested, every Catholic church in the state announced that they are going to fast and pray until this good man is released, and they have been faithful to this promise. Local observers say the country will never be the same.

※ ※ ※ ※ ※

God is always up to something, as my colleague David Redding said years ago in the title of his intriguing book. We just have a hard time seeing God's hand through our immediate tears.

---

world.With hundreds of local residents attesting to Queno's innocence, the judge has told the D.A., "Surely the whole town can't be wrong."

Seven months I lay in bed when I was five, a victim of rheumatic fever, as I related to you in Chapter 1. At the time, for all of us involved, it seemed to be an affliction. A tragedy. I'm sure my mother cried an ocean of tears. I didn't like it any better. But I can look back some fifty years later and say without doubt that those days that seemed so bleak changed my life in almost every way for good. Because of that illness I made choices and went down paths I otherwise would not have elected. Now I know that God had blessings in store for me that I likely would have missed if I never had been sick. God was up to something, but like Paul as he flinched under the jailer's whip, and like Queno when he was led away in handcuffs, I couldn't see it at the moment. Only later, much later, could I see the grace God was bestowing on my family through my pain and weakness.

A close friend lost his home and his job at an age when most folks expect those things to be secure. It hurt me to hear the embarrassment in his voice as this independent, highly skilled man confided that he had been forced into bankruptcy. I know he wanted to cry. And I wanted to cry with him. Right at a stage when it seemed hardest to do, he had to uproot his family. Right when his wisdom and leadership seemed most needed, the church he had ably led lost his shepherding. From every vantage point his situation looked like a disaster. From every vantage point, that is, except God's. God had plans for the man that none of us could see. Our grief and shock kept us from seeing at the time that God was positioning this man to use his talents and his leadership to touch more lives than any of us could ever have dreamed. Far more than he could have blessed in his previous circumstances. God was up to something all along, but that's hard to see when you're praying you won't see anybody you know in the bankruptcy court.

I could tell you dozens of tales like this, of course. The Bible is full of them. Do you suppose Joseph had even an inkling that God was guiding things as he trudged that awful day toward Egypt in slave chains, or when he rotted away in a foreign jail, falsely accused by a no-good woman of things he never even thought of doing? Did he have any way to know in those bleak days that God was getting him positioned to save the world — his family included — from starvation? I doubt it. Years later he could tell his brothers, "You meant it for evil, but God meant it for good." But the hand of God wasn't that visible early on. Not for him. Nor for most of us.

Can we learn anything from all this about proper attitudes during the hard times in our lives? Do the experiences of Paul and Queno and Joseph say anything to us about expecting to see God's light when darkness temporarily obliterates our world? Is it possible that in your life today, right now in the midst of unbearable anguish and pain, God is up to something?

A God who can transform the nails in his hands and the stripes on his back into salvation for a world can turn our own worst experiences into goodness and grace. Of all people, we who worship at the foot of a cross ought to recognize that truth, shouldn't we?

Beauty Among the Ruins

It's gone now, but the ruins of an uncompleted house stood for years at the top of the hill on Earl Garrett Street in the little town where I grew up.

As a 10-year-old newspaper carrier, I was fascinated by those river-rock walls, reaching so uselessly skyward with no rafters or roof ever erected upon them and with no windows or doors ever hung in the empty frames.

It was a home-dreamed, homemade house. Obviously the project of an ambitious soul who selected the most picturesque plot of land overlooking the entire town.

Had the dreamer completed his labors, the house surely would have been a mansion. But his health failed. Or his wealth vanished. Or his life ended. I never knew which.

By the time I came along live oak trees were beginning to grow up inside the walls, and tall weeds covered the lot inside and outside the structure.

I always thought the empty window frames looked like the eye sockets of a skull. Hollow. Stark. Dead.

Nestled in the shadows just west of the huge unfinished house was a tiny hovel. In it lived Mrs. Turner, the spritely widow of the man who had started building her a palace so many years ago.

Smoke from her wood stove curled upward from the chimney of her shanty all winter long, and Mrs. Turner seldom ventured outside.

One April afternoon, however, I found this quiet little lady revelling in the return of the sun's springtime luster as she stood daubing oil paint from palette to canvas, expertly capturing the glory of the zinnias which graced her cottage.

If I would be quiet (no small assignment for a 10-year-old), and if I would stay out of her precious light, she would let me stand for long moments watching her deft strokes as she transferred the transient beauty of the flower petals to the more lasting scene on her easel.

At the time I was mesmerized by her skills with the oil-based hues. Looking back now in my memories, I am even more struck by the ability of that tiny lady to look beyond the shadows of those never-to-be-finished walls and to focus unflinchingly on the beauty that remained in her world.

She was living proof that "weeping tarries for the night, but joy comes in the morning."

The Christmas Funeral

Rob Jeffers was a good funeral director. Probably the best I've ever known. So I was pleased to hear his voice when I answered the church phone late that afternoon. It was less than a week until Christmas and I knew I needed to be getting home. Nita and I still had last minute shopping to do for some of the relatives.

"Preacher," Rob greeted me, "can you help me?"

"What's up, Rob?"

"I hate to bother you this late in the day, but I've got a tough one," he apologized. Then he explained to me quickly that a social worker at the Emergency Room in one of the larger Phoenix hospitals had just called him. Less than an hour ago an ambulance had brought in a 27-year-old white female suffering a severe asthma attack complicated by advanced pneumonia. Shortly after arriving at the hospital, the woman had died.

According to the ambulance attendants and the police, the woman's husband was at home caring for their children. An apartmentful of them.

"The husband and the kids don't know she's dead yet," Rob told me. "And with Christmas so close and the family so poor, the social worker says they hated to just send the cops back out there with a message like this. So they called me.

"The funeral homes in the Valley take turns handling charity funerals," Rob explained to me. "The hospital has the list, so they knew this one would be ours. And they thought I might know a minister who could help break the news to that poor man and his kids."

"And sure enough you did. . ." I jabbed Rob.

"Can you go out there with me?" he begged. "They live out in the low-income housing project. Out in those shabby tan-brick apartments on West Roosevelt."

I knew the place. Far too well. I'd been there often to assist destitute families with various needs, but never one quite like this. I agreed to rendezvous with Rob at the southeast corner of the complex. Then we would go together into the center of the housing project to hunt for the right apartment. It was not the sort of territory anybody ought to be traversing alone. Certainly not at this time of evening. And not if he was white.

Thankfully, the apartment we were looking for was only two rows in from the street. And the last rays of winter sunlight still lingered in the western sky. The sun was vanishing, though, and with it, its warmth. In Arizona nobody but snowbirds and other foreigners own winter clothing, so Rob and I felt the December cold biting through our flimsy suits. I was shivering by the time we reached the door marked 237-B.

Rob pushed the button and inside we heard the clang of a cheap single-note doorbell. A haggard fellow cracked open the door and obviously hesitated when he saw us. What would you do if you answered the door barefoot in khaki pants and a dirty undershirt and found two strangers in fancy suits and ties standing on your doorstep? A toddler shoved his head between Daddy's knee and the door to see who was out there. Milling around behind him we could see several other kids, stair-stepped from about nine to three, it looked like.

"Are you Rusty Barnett?" we asked him.

"Yeah."

"Could you step outside and visit with us for just a moment?" Rob asked. "It won't take but a minute, but we think we should talk to you without the kids listening in."

Rusty Barnett wasn't the sharpest guy in town, but I think he knew by now what we had come to tell him. "Let me get my shoes and my coat," he replied, and closed the door against the winter chill. In a few seconds he slipped outside, telling his oldest daughter to watch the little ones while he was gone. Pressed against the window alongside the door, I could see the noses of three little urchins trying to see what these dressed-up strangers on the front porch wanted with their father.

We introduced ourselves and told Rusty our grim news. He nodded, but said nothing. Fighting for control, he reached out a big raw hand to grip my right shoulder. Putting his other hand on Rob's left shoulder to steady himself, he hung his head as silent sobs wracked his body. I don't suppose we stood like that for more than three or four minutes, but it seemed like hours. Finally Rusty choked back his anguish and asked us, "Will you help me tell my kids?" We nodded. That's what we'd come for.

Inside of the living room of the small apartment it was stifling. A space heater in one corner was turned up full-blast. No wonder Rusty had been stripped down to his undershirt, I thought. My mid-weight suit had been too thin for the cold outside. Inside it was way too heavy. A straggly Christmas tree against one wall took up almost all the navigable space in the tiny room. It looked like a cull the manager at the supermarket tree lot had discarded in the dumpster. A single strand of lonesome lights was all the weight the sagging branches could handle. I wondered. Had Rusty's dead wife decorated that tree? Had she done the best she could on a welfare budget to add this little bit of cheer to their Christmas?

If it is true that wisdom is born of experience, that was a night to make me wise. Nothing they taught me at school and nothing I'd done in my four short years of ministry had prepared me for the conversation I had with Rusty Barnett's children that evening. I don't remember exactly what I said to them. I do know that the God who promised to give his spokesmen words of defense before kings and governors must also provide words for fledgling ministers to speak in comforting motherless children. I certainly had not studied or rehearsed the message I delivered to those children that night. Two-year-old Todd clung to my knee as I talked quietly to the older children. Nine-year-old Sonja and 8-year-old Jeffry pressed close on each side of their weeping father, nodding numbly when I asked if they understood what I was telling them. But it was the 6-year-old, Judd, who grabbed my heart. "You mean Mama won't be here for Christmas?" he asked me plaintively. "We had a present for her!" he sobbed. All five kids turned toward the tree, where 4-year-old Terah picked up a tiny package and showed it to me. Topped with a small red bow, it looked like it had been wrapped by a first grader, with all the love he could muster for his mother. I never did know what trinket they had scrimped to buy for her. Neither did she.

The week before Christmas is a hard time for a funeral. Especially for one like this, when death came so intrusively, so out of season. When we're old and weak, when we've worn out our bodies and used up our days, Death seems somehow more acceptable, doesn't it? But everything inside us cries out when Death encroaches on youth.

When it stops busy life in mid-stride.

When it dares to intrude on Christmas.

I could count on one hand the friends who gathered that morning, just three days before Christmas, to help Rusty and his older children say goodbye to their wife and mother. No preacher can do a very good job of burying a stranger, but I felt more inadequate than ever that morning. How do you comfort people who have no visible tie to the church? A preacher's words are a poor substitute for the hugs and embraces of people who love us in Christ. And how, I wondered, could a preacher address grief in days that are usually filled with joy? I'm not sure I did a very good job that day.

※ ※ ※ ※ ※

Perhaps it would not have changed the funeral I preached for Rusty Barnett's young wife, but I did find out later how to hold a Christmas funeral.

Here in Amarillo, nine or ten years after the events I
just related to you, my friend Walker Bateman lost a
teenaged son in the days right before Christmas. A host
of friends gathered in the large sanctuary of First
Presbyterian Church, most of us feeling keenly the
dissonance between youth and death that I've just
described. Because of their own deep trust in Christ,
however, the Bateman family instructed their pastor to
make that funeral service a celebration of faith. In doing
so, they blessed us all.

I will never forget Dr. Jim Carroll's opening words
that afternoon. He shocked us when he called us to
worship by affirming with the psalmist, *"This is the day
the Lord has made. Let us rejoice, and be glad in it!"*

Let us do *what*? I recoiled at first. This is a funeral!

With a beneficent smile, however, that great man of
God proclaimed that Jesus came to Bethlehem to
conquer sorrow and to give us Life. One by one he
reminded us of the words of the great carols of
Christmas. Familiar words, like

> *Hark! the herald angels sing,*
> *Glory to the newborn King! . . .*

Had we ever noticed before that a later verse of this
carol says,

> *Mild He lays His glory by,*
> *Born that man no more may die,*
> *Born to raise the sons of earth,*
> *Born to give them second birth.*

We Christians traditionally look to Easter for resurrection, but Christmas is also God's answer to death.
Christmas is also his antidote to grief. God sent forth
his Son "to comfort all who mourn," the prophet wrote

(Isaiah 61). In this second funeral I'm telling you about, we claimed that comfort. We countered grief with the joy of Christmas. So the choir that day sang,

> *Good Christian men, rejoice*
> *With heart and soul and voice.*
> *Now ye need not fear the grave:*
> *Peace! Peace!*
> *Jesus Christ was born to save.*

Our Lord came to undo all that Adam did to us, Jim Carroll assured us in his funeral message that day. All the curses that fell on Eden were undone by the One who came to die on Calvary. So through tears that day we sang,

> *Joy to the world! the Lord is come;*
> *Let earth receive her King.*
> *Let ev'ry heart prepare Him room,*
> *And heav'n and nature sing. . .*

And we affirmed in Verse 3 of this favorite carol:

> *No more let sin and sorrow grow,*
> *Nor thorns infest the ground,*
> *He comes to make His blessings flow*
> *Far as the curse is found.*

Lifting our voices together that day, we acknowledged the grand truth of Romans 5 that the Child born in Bethlehem repaired all the damage done to our world by the inhabitants of Eden. And together we prayed in song,

> *O come, O come, Emmanuel,*
> *And ransom captive Israel,*
> *That mourns in lowly exile here*
> *Until the Son of God appear.*

> *O come, Thou Dayspring, come and cheer*
> *Our spirits by Thine advent here.*

Disperse the gloomy clouds of night,
And death's dark shadows put to flight.

Rejoice! Rejoice! Emmanuel
Shall come to thee, O Israel!

So we that day, the Israel of God, unexpectedly found healing for our broken hearts in the story of Bethlehem.

From dozens of churches all over our city, we gathered that day a thousand strong and obeyed a Bible command we usually ignore. For one precious hour we forgot our differences, and, as Romans 15:6 commands, "with one heart and mouth" we glorified "the God and Father of our Lord Jesus Christ."

O come, let us adore Him!

our voices and hearts sang together,

O come, let us adore Him —
Christ, the Lord!

We left that Christmas funeral with our souls uplifted, our hearts warmed, because we had tasted anew the goodness of the Good News that began in Bethlehem.

Life after Divorce

Is there really life after divorce?

The answer to this question depends on who you ask, and on what stage they may be in as they deal with the grief that inevitably follows the death of a marriage.

The experts today are rethinking the pat answers offered a generation ago about the damage done by divorce. For more than three decades counselors parroted the widely accepted nonsense that divorce was a temporary trauma that need not leave lasting scars on the mates involved and fewer still on their kids. Today, however, counselors are seeing too many angry people to ignore them, people who 20 or 30 years later still are angry about deep hurts they suffered when their world came apart — when their family disintegrated — usually due to circumstances they as children could not control. As we listen to the pain-filled tales of these victims, we are finally catching up with the wisdom of our Creator, who said centuries ago, "I hate divorce." Now we know why.

But the God who hated it, allowed it. Longing to save us and our children from the brokenness that follows divorce, from the beginning God set up the ideal of lifelong marriage. One man/one woman, for all their days. But, unlike some of us who claim to speak for him, God is a realist. He knows that in a fallen world made up of imperfect human beings, some marriages will fail and the people involved will be hurt. Today we live with that reality in the church. Hardly a family has escaped the devastation of divorce. Whether we like it or not, it's here. Like gravity. Trying to act like it doesn't exist is a good way for us to bump our heads. Latest figures show that fewer than half of America's children live in a home with both their natural parents. The rest live in homes that are mixed, blended, single-parent, foster. The church will not bless these families by endlessly railing against the evils they have already endured. They need us to tell them instead about God's grace and love and hope for today. That is my purpose in the pages that follow.

* * * * *

To help you see God's goodness, I want to tell you a story. Before I begin, though, let me assure you that if, as I go along, you think I'm telling your story, or maybe your daughter's or your granddaughter's, you're wrong. I would not do that to you. If we have prayed together and wept together about troubles in your life, you never have to be afraid that your confidences might show up in a book or sermon someday. Sadly, however, the true tale I'm about to unfold is indeed the story of dozens of Christians across our land.

* * * * *

Dirty dishes were piled precariously in the sink. Cracker crumbs and coffee grounds and last week's Rice Krispies defiled a kitchen cabinet stacked haphazardly with empty tuna fish cans, half-full cereal boxes, and stale remnants of bread loaves partially consumed in the two weeks just past. Jan Thomas understood Matthew's observation that they gathered up twelve basketfuls of leftovers after Jesus fed the crowd. It seemed to her that most of the jumble and junk that made her house so depressing was the result of some meal she and the kids had eaten three days ago and then forgotten to clean up after.

In the pre-dawn moments before the kids roused, Jan fought back tears as she sat at one end of the rickety antique-green table in the corner of her tiny kitchen. She was nursing a cup of instant Folgers. No need to brew real coffee anymore. Now that she's the only coffee drinker in the house. *I'll need to pick up another jar of coffee when I'm at Albertson's,* Jan thought, *if I can squeeze it into the food budget. Maybe I ought to quit drinking it altogether. It is one thing we don't just have to have. Strange how many "necessities" the kids and I have learned to get along without since Glenn left. I bet he's got all the money he needs for coffee. Probably blows more for coffee every day at the cafe than it costs me to buy this instant yuck for a month.*

As she re-convinced herself of the unfairness of her meager circumstances for the umpteenth time in recent days, tears tumbled out, splashing on the permanently

stained table top. She'd cried so much since Glenn had
gone. By now she thought she would have run out of
tears, but how do you not cry when the person you
planned to spend your life with has decided he loves
somebody else's wife, and all the plans you made, the
dreams you dreamed, the comforts the two of you had
slowly accumulated in 18 years of marriage have gone
poof. Evaporated. Like they never existed. And while
he plays with his Sweet-Young-Thing, enjoying the
financial freedom of her income on top of his high
salary, you struggle alone to put together pennies for
school lunches and day care and dentist bills and laun-
dry soap. Not to mention rent on a run-down apartment, and shoes for Tommy (whose feet seem to grow
two inches a month these days), and insurance for the
car. Jan was thankful for the HMO at her new job.
Without it she didn't know what they would do.

I've got to stop letting myself be so miserable, Jan
scolded herself when a tear splattered on her coffee-
cup-holding hand. *It's not fair to the kids for me to stay in a
funk all the time,* she thought. *But how do you laugh when
you want to scream curses? Why try to smile, when your
smile looks more like a whimper?* Jan rose from the table
and began poking around in the cabinets, wondering if
they had anything she could fix for breakfast instead of
letting the kids drag out the cold cereal for themselves
as they had now for weeks. She knew finding hot
breakfast on the table would surprise them. Maybe perk
them up a little and brighten their day. But what could
she fix? She remembered that her mom used to bake
scratch biscuits and make flour gravy when the budget
was tight and flour was all they had in the house, but
Jan had no idea how to transform flour into bread. Her

biscuits came from a can. At least they did back when they could afford them. Rummaging through the pantry she came across a half-used box of pancake mix she'd long since forgotten. A quick scan of the fridge turned up the necessary two eggs and enough milk in the bottom of the jug to make the batter (with just a little water added in). Now where in the world in this disastrous kitchen could she find a clean pan?

It probably would have shocked Jan Thomas to know how many women in her city started off their morning much as she did that day. Same hurt. Same worries. Same anger. Same tears. Right then she couldn't see it. Her own tears blinded her to anybody else's pain. The weariness of long work hours, her impossible budget crunch, and her never-ending single-parent duties made it hard for Jan to think clearly even about her own responsibilities. Straining to the limit to meet her own obligations narrowed her focus to her own troubles and made them seem even more insurmountable than they really were.

"Please call Jan Thomas and urge her to bring the kids to the Christmas party," I asked one of our church ladies. I knew Jan would probably think she was too tired, too broke, too ashamed, to attend such a function unless we pushed a little. "Tell her we've bought a few extra presents her kids can use as their special gifts to the widows." Two dollars doesn't seem like much for a Christmas gift. Multiply that times Jan's three kids and you would come up with six dollars I knew she simply didn't have. What a shame! I thought. For years Jan and Glenn had been some of our most generous people in planning church activities, often providing the "extra" others couldn't afford. Now Glenn was gone and Jan felt like a bum if she came to Christmas dinner at church without bringing food for the table or gifts for the tree. What we planned as a festive occasion of good will and cheer for our congregation probably loomed as a grim challenge to Jan's new poverty. Our fun could so easily become her gloom; our joy in a happy season, a reason for deepening depression and melancholy in Jan. So several of us that year took special pains to be sure our celebration of Christmas blessed Jan instead of wounding her fragile heart.

*****

"Can I visit with you?" Jan asked when she called me at the church a few weeks later.

"Sure. What would be a good time for you?" We mulled over our calendars and set a time on Thursday in between her lunch hour and the time she had to pick up Tina at school to take her to the orthodontist.

Jan looked better now than she had in those forlorn days right after Glenn had ditched her. Some of the shock was wearing off, I guess. She and the kids were adjusting to their new routines, and Jan's natural resourcefulness was slowly reviving, it seemed. But she was still a long way from what you would call "happy."

"If only I had not been such a dummy," Jan spluttered as we talked about her situation. "If only I had known Glenn was fooling around. If only. . ."

Too much of Jan's mental energy was being drained uselessly in her daily litany of "if only's." I tried to help her see that. "'If only,'" I told her, "is the password into a fairy tale, into a fantasy land. It didn't exist then, and it never will. It's a place where we go to wallow in guilt for things we probably weren't to blame for in the first place."

Jan was a smart lady. Now that she was beginning to think clearly again, she instantly grasped what I was telling her. With just a little coaching she was sharp enough to catch herself when she slipped back into the "if only" doldrums and in the days ahead she would force herself instead to think useful, productive thoughts.

"You really don't think the divorce was my fault, do you?" Somehow this surprised Jan.

"No, Jan." I assured her. "I'm sure you and Glenn had some rough times in your marriage, like everybody does. I'm sure there were days when you were less than lovable. All of us have those days. Right now, in your grief, those are the days you tend to remember. But those stormy times were the normal ups and downs of a marriage. They did not cause your divorce."

Jan was listening. She wanted to believe what I was telling her, but the guilt that always goes with grief held her back.

"Jan," I pressed the point, "even if we accept the obvious truth that you were not always perfect, you did not cause your divorce. You honored your vows. You loved your husband. You provided a good home. You cared for your family. Jan, I've known you long enough and well enough to know that you were doing what a Christian wife is supposed to do. And nothing you did or did not do caused Glenn to get infatuated with that gal at the office. He would love for you to assume the blame for the sin he committed, but it was his sin, not yours, that ended your marriage. You need to accept this, because it is the truth that will set you free."

I noticed that tears were sliding down Jan's cheeks. And she nodded, knowing I had just told her the truth.

Some months later when I visited again with Jan, she had obviously turned a corner in her recovery. The renewed happiness in her soul shone clearly in her spontaneous smile. "Last week," she told me, "the kids and I made it home to Springfield to see Mom and Dad for the first time since Glenn left us. The Lord's timing was marvelous. We went to church with my folks Sunday morning, and God planned the sermon just for me."

"He does that for us sometimes," I agreed. "What did you hear that blessed you so much?"

"The preacher there where Mom and Dad worship had been giving a series of lessons on dealing with death. The sermon we heard Sunday was on grief recovery. Although Glenn isn't dead, almost everything the preacher said fit my situation."

"And you found it helpful."

"You bet! I don't always remember sermons," Jan confessed, and then she snickered, "Not even yours. But I'll never forget the three things he said God does to help us recover from grief."

"Which were. . . ?" I led her.

"First," Jan held up her right forefinger, "he said *God forgives us*. God takes away all the guilt grieving people dredge up to abuse themselves with. 'The blood of Jesus cleanses us from *every* sin,' he insisted. Even the ones we imagine. Any wrong we may think we have done is covered by God's grace. 'There's no condemnation to those of us who are in Christ,' the Bible teaches, so we must not spend our days condemning ourselves."

"Did he use the other great Romans verse? The one that says, 'Since we are justified by faith, we have peace with God'?"

"Yes! And I knew as he quoted it that I've found that peace again in my own heart."

Jan raised another finger to signal sermon point Number Two. "To help us get over grief, the preacher said, *God also empowers us.* He talked about how much the apostle Paul had given up to follow Christ, what a tremendous sense of loss he must have felt. But Paul said, 'I can do everything through him who gives me strength.' We can, too." Jan smiled confidently as she affirmed her own capability. Then she added, "I especially appreciated his remarks about the role the Holy Spirit plays in grief recovery. He pointed us to several Scriptures, like the one in Romans 8 that says, 'The Spirit helps us in our weakness.'" For a split second Jan paused. "You know," she reflected, "now that I'm learning to cope again, I look back and I'm amazed at how helpless I felt in those first days. The preacher in Springfield certainly was right. The Lord *has* given me strength."

Probably imitating the preacher she had heard the week before, Jan now held up three fingers on her right hand. Pointing to her ring finger, she told me, "Point Number Three in the sermon was that *God restores us* after we've been broken. I loved the verse he cited from 1 Peter about God putting us back together after we suffer —"

"— the one that says, 'The God of all grace, who called you to his eternal glory in Christ, after you have suffered a little while, will himself restore you and make you strong'?"

"Yeah," Jan beamed, "that's the one. Isn't that a great thought, that when we've been damaged by life's disasters — like I was — God provides healing to make us whole again?"

As Jan started out the door, she turned and said, "You know, that preacher in Springfield didn't say anything I didn't know all along, but those truths spoke to my heart Sunday morning in a special way. Glenn's not dead, of course. Sometimes I've thought it might have been easier for the kids and me if he was. But we lost him anyway, and we lost the life our marriage made possible. For all of those losses we have grieved. I'm so grateful to God for helping me get through it so we can start living again."

✳ ✳ ✳ ✳ ✳

Well, that's my tale. I know that in our fellowship we're not used to hearing women preach, but I wanted you to hear Jan's story because I wanted you to hear that sermon she repeated. It's a great one, full of truths we all need to hear when life comes apart on us and we're hurting bad. We need to know that instead of blaming us for our problems,

➤ *God forgives us*
➤ *God empowers us*
➤ *God restores us*

because of the love He has for us in Christ Jesus. If this is true, then divorce, however tragic, is not the end. Through God's grace, its victims can live whole and happy lives again.

The Glory That
Will Be Revealed

I consider that our present sufferings are not worth comparing with the glory that will be revealed in us (Romans 8:18).

The evening before we lost my mother, I sat alone with her and we talked. Beyond that night she would survive physically for eight dreadful months, but except for rare flickerings of clarity, she was not really "there" after that evening. That night I broke the hospital's rule against visitors sitting on a patient's bed. The head of Mom's bed was tilted high, and she slid over to one side so I could sit down near the resulting bend in the mattress, my left hip beside hers, facing her. I held her hands in mine as we visited quietly. By some stroke of heaven's mercy, we were alone for that hour. Until then it had been a hectic day, a day spent racing to the radiologist's office, hurrying back to the hospital to catch her doctor, answering dozens of phone calls from family and friends, shuttling in and out of Mom's room, more to reassure ourselves than to do her any material good. Now the rest of the family had drifted away at supper time, and she and I enjoyed a blessed hour. Just us together. "Use these moments wisely," something (or Someone?) said inside me. It was a valid warning, for this turned out to be the last real conversation I had with my mother. In the awful days that followed we did talk. We exchanged bits of verbal communication. But after that night she was seldom there in the body we cared for. Instead we talked in those days to a stranger conjured up by chemical injections and by brain tissues mashed by a growing malignancy and cooked by radiation. So I will always treasure that last lucid hour with my mom when she and I talked almost nonchalantly about things dear to both of us.

"Tell me about Grandpa Key when you were a little girl," I led her. Leaving that Houston hospital room, at least in spirit, we trudged briefly together through the mesquite and prickly pear thickets of Coke County in West Texas. Despite her tiredness, her eyes danced as she shared childhood memories of incidents we somehow had failed to discuss in 50-plus years of mother/son chatter. Soon, I realized, these memories would be lost forever, so I kept questioning. Probing. Hungry to hear more. Sadly I must confess that most of the details she shared with me that evening soon faded into the blur of shock and grief that shrouded those days. I remember now only a few smatterings of what she told me that night about my great-grandparents, but I will never forget her immense pleasure in recounting those memories.

"Was Grandpa Key a Christian?" I asked her. "Was

he a believer?" I knew her mother's people were. Somewhat fanatically so, I remembered. My Great-granddad Shropshire was a Bible-thumping legalist with a passion to proselyte his neighbors or, if they resisted, to confess their sins. But Great-grandpa Key had a quieter, kinder faith. Not one, I suppose, that would pass muster when judged by the Keepers of Orthodoxy, but a faith my dying mother remembered seven decades later as being far more charitable and much more Christlike than the stricter approach of the ones who judged her Grandpa unfit for the Kingdom. Talking with Mom that night in the hospital gave me fresh insight into why she, and her children after her, have been somewhat impatient with much of the nonsense church folks do in Jesus' name.

Discussing our ancestors' faith that evening caused Mom and me to talk briefly about our own. My mother was a realist, and even before the diagnosis of her brain tumor was complete, her training as a nurse made her only too aware of the ordeal she was facing. "I don't want a lot of heroic efforts made to keep me here," she said matter-of-factly. "There are worse things than dying."

About that time we heard her door open, and a voice called, "Mrs. Shelburne?" I turned to see a nurse with a larger than usual hypodermic syringe in her hand. She glowered at me for sitting on Mom's bed and motioned for me to get out of her way. "I have some medication the doctor has ordered for you."

Surprised at the size of the dosage, I asked her what it was for. She explained that the doctor was concerned that Mom's growing brain tumor at any moment might trigger a new round of violent nausea, or maybe even seizures. Whatever the drug was, its stated purpose was to shrink the brain tissue and thus to delay the inevitable symptoms. It did. But it caused worse. Within 20 minutes, Mom was absolutely wild. Nothing we said would stop her tears. Nothing we did would calm her fears. All evening she struggled and wailed. In that frantic state, she was wheeled from ICU to an unfamiliar room in another part of the building, thus aggravating the distress of her disorientation. It was almost midnight when she finally slipped into a fitful sleep and the nurses insisted that we leave her in their care.

For the creation was subjected to frustration.

If the events in my mother's hospital room later that night had not been so tragic, they would have been hilarious.

The old lady who shared the room with my mother that night was a completely disoriented Alzheimer's patient who moaned non-stop, every few moments yelling, "Nurse! Nurse!" loudly enough to be heard in the next county. And the nurses, having more than they could do just to care for their sane patients and knowing this poor lady was out of her gourd, for the most part ignored her cries. They had her poseyed to the bed — tied down — for her own safety, so they just let her lie there and holler.

What the nurses failed to reckon on that night was the nurse in the bed next to this poor lady. Neither the ICU staff nor the doctor had paid enough attention to us to know how totally Mom had flipped out after they medicated her. So they had not tied her down. At least not to start with. So Mom was free to roam and ramble.

Way in the night her roommate's pitiful cries for a nurse penetrated my mother's medicated brain, and the nurse in her responded. Just what Mom intended to do to help her distressed neighbor none of us could ever figure out, but she climbed out of bed in the 2:00 a.m. darkness, clawed her way through the curtain that separated the two beds, staggered into the maze of tubes and wires connected to the Alzheimer's patient, and then fell. Dizzy and drunk from the brain shrinking chemicals, my mother rolled and twisted and fought the medical machines and paraphernalia that seemed to be keeping her pinned to the floor. Can you imagine the reaction of the nurses who found her — who knows how much later? — with her own IV lines hopelessly snarled and fouled with her roommate's? On an already too busy night, it took the nurses hours to repair the havoc. In her confused state, all my mother remembered the next day was that as the nurses sorted out the spaghetti of tubes and tangled wires, they scolded her relentlessly and then tied her into her bed, as they should have to begin with.

When Dad and the rest of us got to the hospital after breakfast the next morning, we knew nothing about any of this, of course. One of Mom's adopted sons (she was always adopting stray boys like puppies) had arrived before us. Stopping by the hospital on his way to work, he had found my mother sobbing her heart out. "I only wanted to help!" she wailed over and over. "I only wanted to help!" When nothing he said could console her, big Steve finally scooped her small body up in his arms. We found him sitting on the side of her bed, holding her and rocking her, trying to soothe her as if she were a frightened little girl. All that morning we took turns, but the trauma and frustration of that awful night had bruised her spirit beyond repair.

Since this is so personally painful, I struggle to communicate plainly. Please do not assume for a minute that I think my mother was singled out for special abuse or suffering. While her hospital care and doctoring during that awful 24 hours was less than stellar, I suspect my tale is tame compared to some of the medical horror stories I hear. What I mean to share with you is not a complaint against the medical system, but, instead, a more general observation of the suffering and soul-pain common to all humanity. "The whole creation has been groaning as in the pains of childbirth right up to the present time," the Scriptures acknowledge. And it's not just the bad folks who hurt. It's not just the farmers who till the sin-cursed soil and the mothers condemned since Eden to bear offspring in agony. All of us groan.

We ourselves, who have the firstfruits of the Spirit, groan inwardly as we wait eagerly for . . .the redemption of our bodies.

To participate in the miracles of modern medicine, my mother paid a hideous price. Diagnostic surgery done with star-wars techniques confirmed our worst fears. The tumor crowding out my mother's healthy brain cells was malignant. Of a sort not likely to respond to treatment. But it's hard to give up, isn't it?

"One of your choices, Mr. Shelburne, is to do nothing," the compassionate young neurosurgeon told my father. More than once. But how do you "do nothing" when it means giving up the one you've loved so faithfully for so many years? So the months that followed were filled with the futility of desperate therapies doomed to fail. Treatments that hurt more than they helped, in fact. My mother cooperated bravely, groaning all the while because of the weakness and pain. But groaning far more, as the Scriptures say, for "the redemption" of her body.

I remember one night when Dad went to the church to teach his Spanish Bible course. By then we never left Mom alone, but I was visiting them for two or three days, so I gladly stayed with her that night. By then, whether because of the tumor's growth or the radiation's damage we never knew, she slept a lot. Whenever she did stir, communication was usually limited to a word or two, or maybe a groan. Except when Dad was gone. Then Mom became quite active and irrationally afraid. Not for herself, but for him. For almost 60 years she had been concerned for her husband's safety, and now, when he left her bedside even for short periods, this concern consumed her. Every two or three minutes she roused to ask me where he was. Was he O.K.? Maybe we should call. Why wasn't he home yet? Had he had an accident? None of my answers satisfied her for long, so I just stood beside her hospital bed there in their tiny living room and held her hand.

That's when she surprised me. Suddenly, with eyes clear and thoughts precise for the first time in weeks, she looked up at me and said, "I'm ready to go. Please pray that God will take me soon." I promised her I would. And moments later she was lost again in a stupor of weakness and fear.

When we're young and healthy and life's coming up roses, most of us don't think much about eternity, do we? Or about hope. We're too caught up in family fun and career achievements, too enamored with present

116

Expect the Light!

pleasures to look very far ahead. But when our used-up bodies consign us to days of weakness and indignity and pain, then, maybe for the first time, we begin to understand and treasure the Christian hope "that the creation itself will be liberated from its bondage to decay and brought into the glorious freedom of the children of God." That's what my mother was longing for.

Release from the now-useless struggle.

Freedom from a body gone bad.

And the glory that awaits all God's children.

Now past the time in life when most of us dread death and secretly hope to live as long as George Burns or Methuselah, my mother had at last reached the stage described in Scripture when God's children "wait eagerly" for him to take them home.

In this hope we were saved.

I'm not sure what the apostle means by "saved" in this line. In church we tend to use the word to describe the Christian conversion experience, using the word in a technical, doctrinal way that makes sense only to those who know the vocabulary of the Kingdom. In Bible days the word used here was far more general. Sometimes it meant to be *healed* of an injury or a disease. More often it meant to *rescue* or to *deliver* someone from danger or harm. On other occasions the same word meant to *preserve* something or to *keep it safe*. I wonder what Paul has in mind when he says in this memorable text that we were "saved *in* (the King James Bible says *by*) this hope."

Is he implying here that when we come to Jesus for *salvation* of our souls (that is another form of the same word, you know), we are laying claim at the very same time to a whole new way of looking at life? A way that sets us free from the cynicism and despair of a Godless view of life and for the first time makes available to us an unquenchable hope. When we start looking at human existence through Jesus' eyes, hope springs to life in us. Without Jesus people live in a dead-end world. This material existence is all there is to it, with its pain and disappointment and mindless agony. When we accept Jesus, we affirm with believers through the centuries that our Lord came from glory in order to take us to glory. He has always *been*, and always will *be*. So his power and love and grace are always available to those who trust in him. In the bleakest hours of life, his love sustains us. In the darkest days, his light of grace shines undimmed. Regardless of our physical circumstances, in Jesus we are never without hope.

"In this hope we were saved," the NIV says. "We were saved by this hope," the King James insists. "In this hope we are saved," the RSV promises. These words of Romans 8:24, so simple and yet so hard to translate, can legitimately convey all of these truths. The hope we obtain in Christian salvation continues from that time on to buoy us up in difficult moments and literally saves us (preserves us, heals us, rescues us) when the tragedies of life would otherwise undo us.

I testify to you that in those days when my mother lay dying, this hope made all the difference.

Fragile!
Handle with Prayer!

With my good friend Ken Lape, on a crisp fall day, I wandered the hills of the Mohawk Valley in central New York, marvelling at Midas-touched meadows of goldenrod and revelling in the bursts of flaming orange and luminous yellow leaves. And I wondered from a West Texan's perspective why God played favorites when he parcelled out trees and streams and greenness in his world.

Like the bush that burned for Moses, one maple beside our path radiated red. "In a week or so," Ken remarked, "the whole countryside will look like this. But," he added wistfully, "when the leaves are prettiest, they're fragile."

A hard freeze, a driving rain, one gusty day can extinguish the blazing leaves, leaving the forest looking gray and dead. Like ashes.

All of life is like that. Fragile. Frighteningly so.

In an unforeseen instant one tiny clot of blood shifting silently in a narrowed artery turned my gifted aerospace technologist friend into a stumbling, half-blind, confused little man, his genius and expertise forever gone.

René Boris was alive as few people are. Vital. Vibrant. She exuded energy and enthusiasm as she scurried about her community on errands of loving, fun-filled mercy. It took only seconds that night five years ago for a drunken driver to force her tiny VW off the road's edge. Over an embankment. Into a tree. Which crumpled her Bug and instantly snuffed out her precious life.

Just as fragile as our bodies are our dreams. Like leaves that glow in today's sunlight only to be trampled into tomorrow's mud, our brightest dreams for marriages, children, or jobs seem ever more likely to be eclipsed. Today nothing seems to be forever, or even for very long, does it?

Faced with such fragility, more than ever our world yearns for something solid and lasting to renew our hope, to calm our fears.

My fellow leaf-gazer, Ken, has found such a stabilizer for his life. Long before his stroke, so did my friend who made aerospace prototypes. Before her needless death, so did lovely René. Each of these good friends discovered that the only sure thing in this fragile world is the unfailing love of an eternal God.

The Morning Star

We have the word of the prophets made more certain, and you will do well to pay attention to it, as to a light shining in a dark place, until the day dawns and the morning star rises in your hearts (2 Peter 1:19).

Imagine that you're a spelunker. A cave explorer. Despite your wisest precautions, your batteries unexplainably fail. All of them. Now your headlamp is dead. Your flashlight is useless. In dangerous underground terrain where your next step might be your last, you are trapped in total darkness. What would you give at this bone-chilling moment to see a light — even a small light — shining into the cavern that could so easily become your grave?

This is how the apostle Peter describes God's word. "A light shining in a dark place." Illumination at a dreadful moment when all the lights we normally count on have flickered and failed.

* * * * *

Saralynn hit a time like that. I mean one when all the
lights seemed to go out and only darkness remained.
She had seen it coming for years but kept telling herself
it wasn't so. The first time Bert blacked her eye she
couldn't believe it. From the earliest days of their dating
back in high school she had known he had a fiery
temper, but he had always kept it in check toward her.
Until that night almost four years ago when he came
home steamed about something at work, and then,
when she begged him not to swear in front of little Jeb,
Bert backhanded her and cursed her with words she
had never heard him use before.

The next morning Bert seemed sorry. "Forgive me!"
he begged her. "I won't ever hit you again." She believed
him. To keep family and church folks from knowing
what had happened, Saralynn stayed close to home for
almost two weeks. Until the angry purple bruises above
and below her right eye quit shining. Until the bruises to
her soul stopped bleeding. Having been raised by a
gentle Christian father who seldom raised his voice and
never raised his hand against his wife or his daughters,
Saralynn had no experience with handling this kind of
mistreatment. She had no way to know that men who
batter their wives almost always repeat their offenses.
Naively she protected her guilty husband and prayed
that these bad days would soon pass.

They did. They got worse.

Three years and another baby later, Saralynn had
lost count of the times Bert had beaten her and then
promised never to do it again. By then her parents and
her sisters knew. Not the worst of it. But they knew Bert
had hurt her more than once. By then Bert was afraid of
the consequences if too many people found out his

dirty little secret, so most of the time he controlled his battering just enough to be sure the injuries he inflicted would be hidden by clothing. In doing this, of course, he tipped his hand. Such cunning betrayed the calculated meanness of his attacks on his wife. Although Saralynn still played the morning-after game of letting him tearfully profess his penitence for damages done the night before, deep in her heart she knew by this time that Bert meant to hurt her. That he *liked* to hurt her. And, although she never said it, she knew that one day he would likely to go too far.

Like so many battered women who suffer silently while their spouses or lovers increase the ferocity of their attacks, Saralynn let Bert turn up the level of abuse without even once looking for outside help. At night she dreaded to hear him coming home from work. Especially when he had to work late. Because those were the nights when he seemed more likely to come unwound. Then the danger for her and the kids was the greatest. Even more, however, she dreaded the idea of being left alone with two kids and no job, no income. At least Bert paid the bills.

"Honey child," her mother pled with her one day, "let us help you find a safe place for you and your babies to live." When Saralynn bent down to pick up the baby, she had winced out loud from the pain of a recent injury from Bert's pounding. Her mother heard the pain and knew the reason.

"Oh, Mom," Saralynn jumped to Bert's defense, "Bert's just under a lot of pressure at work these days. Anyway, lots of it's my fault. I should know better than to upset him when he's already stressed out." A strange common denominator links abused wives. Almost all of them allow their no-good husbands to convince them that the abuse they suffer is deserved. That the blame belongs to the victim. Saralynn was no exception.

She drove back home that evening more torn up inside than ever. Her mother's spoken concerns verified her own rising fears that she and the children were in real danger. But she felt trapped. And guilty. *"What God has joined together, let no man separate."* She knew that Bible verse. *"Anyone who divorces. . ., except for marital unfaithfulness, and marries another. . .commits adultery."* All of her life Saralynn had heard preachers quote those words, and she believed them. The very thought that her marriage might fail was anathema to her. No way! Not on your life! She would find a way to make it work. Even if it killed her.

So this frightened, hurting Christian lady did exactly what her spiritual training had taught her to do. When things got tough, she prayed more. She prayed harder. And she began to search her Bible, looking urgently for strength and insight to make her world O.K. again. Lost in the darkest cave of her life, she frantically sought for light. And she was not disappointed. *"Those who hope in the Lord will renew their strength,"* Isaiah promised her. With David she learned to pray, *"The Lord is my light and my salvation — whom shall I fear?"* How ironic, I thought when I first heard Saralynn's story — how ironic that in her desperation she was both *trapped* by Scripture and *sustained* by Scripture! Have you ever been there? The apostle Peter was right, however. The word of God provided Saralynn the only light she saw during those dark days of loneliness and abuse and pain. For her, God's word was indeed "a light shining in a dark place."

Finally, A Way Out

Saralynn's parents knew something was wrong when she called one afternoon months later. Her voice was subdued, they told me. She was almost whispering into the telephone.

"How are you, honey?" they inquired.

Tears and sobs were their answer. In the background they heard two voices, male and female, urging Saralynn to tell them, assuring her that she *could* tell them. Before she managed to speak a word her parents smiled to one another. They just knew that the Lord had finally answered their often-repeated prayers for him to send someone to rescue their daughter.

"Bert hasn't been coming home at night much for a long time." Saralynn poured out her words of grief when she got through crying. "He lost his job several weeks ago, so I had to find one. He's been drawing unemployment and spending most of his time fiddling with old cars at a friend's wrecking yard. At 6:00 this morning he came home. Right when I was leaving for work. I never did know for sure what he asked me while I was pouring his coffee. It was something about where he had parked the car — "

Sobs choked off her words again. And again Saralynn's parents heard the voices of their daughter's helpers, whoever they were, comforting and encouraging her.

" — Bert grabbed me," she resumed her tale. "He forced me back against the cabinet and choked me until I almost passed out. Then he let me go and mumbled something about teaching me to answer him right."

Through intermittent torrents of tears Saralynn told her parents she had managed to snatch up the two kids,

grab a bag of clothes she had packed for them, and
escape with the two boys to the home of the elderly
couple who had been babysitting them most of their
lives. For many months they had been aware of Bert's
abusive behavior, and had pled with Saralynn to leave
him, so they were quick to recognize the danger and
eager to protect the children. Fearful of losing her rela-
tively new job and already late, Saralynn hurried off to
work. She had hardly clocked in, though, when she
realized that Bert probably would come looking for her
there. "If you ever try to leave me," he had raged in
recent days, "I'll take the kids where you and your kin
will never find 'em, and I'll kill you." From the experiences of the morning she knew he was angry enough
and crazy enough to do just that. So, apologizing to her
boss, she clocked back out, and hurried to retrieve the
kids before Bert came looking for them.

Where would she go with them? Already a plan was
forming. At church she had made two new friends, Jim
and Terri Smith, who had moved back home to Laramie
to care for her elderly mother. She knew they would
take her in, and she doubted Bert would even know
about them. He hadn't been to church since he lost his
job, so he had not met them. Surprised at first by their
unexpected appearance, Jim and Terri welcomed
Saralynn and her brood. He heard only the first part of
her tearful story before he asked for her car keys. "We
need to get your car off the street," he explained. "Bert
might spot it." Quickly he pulled her old Toyota into
the vacant side of their large garage and closed the
metal door. Bert would never guess it was there.

Jim and Terri were the people Saralynn's parents
heard when she called that morning. Realizing that

Saralynn was too shaken to think clearly, they encouraged her to let her family know what was happening. When the call was done, Jim led Saralynn to Step #2.

"Are you sure you want out of this mess?" Jim asked her.

"Yes," Saralynn nodded. "But I'm afraid of what Bert will do. If he finds out you guys have helped me, he might even hurt you."

"Let me worry about that," Jim countered as he dialed the number of an attorney who had helped them on the sales contract for their new house. By mid-afternoon divorce papers had been filed and the judge had granted a restraining order against Bert. Then Jim and Terri loaded up Saralynn and the boys and transported them two hours away to an isolated farmhouse where some of Terri's cousins lived in a neighboring state.

"Where is my wife?" Bert blustered the next morning when he called Saralynn's parents. They were able to tell him truthfully that they didn't know. "She ain't gonna get away with this," he screamed. "She's got my boys!" With mushrooming threats and obscenities he lacerated those good people for several long minutes. Finally they hung up on him and let him curse lamely into their answering machine on his repeated attempts to call back. Realizing that a man so wildly out of control had to be drunk or doped up, they elected to pray for him instead of trying to give sensible answers to his irrational demands.

Deeper Into the Cave

It took Bert less than a month to find Saralynn. A month that her parents described as an emotional roller coaster ride for them. Imagine how they felt, for example, when they heard that Saralynn's former boss had taken his family on an extended vacation to protect them from Bert's insane anger. Bert was so out of control that he even dared to threaten the judge who issued the restraining order against him. At one moment Saralynn's parents would be thanking God for getting her and the grandkids out of harm's way. In the next moment they would be anxiously pleading with the Almighty to keep Bert from making good on his threats to kill them and anybody else he suspected of shielding Saralynn.

Any fears they had for themselves were diverted when news came that Saralynn and the boys had vanished. Somehow Bert learned where they were hiding. Sheriff's deputies found her abandoned car a few miles north of the farm. They theorized that in some way she must have discovered that Bert was closing in and she tried to get away. All of her belongings, including all the kids' clothing, were left behind in the farmhouse. She took only her purse and the boys and fled. A statewide alert failed to turn up a trace of Saralynn and the children. Lawmen soon widened the search nationwide, but three weeks later no one had seen or heard from Bert and his terrified family. Authorities feared the worst.

What do you do when the people who are dearest to you are in grave danger, and you're many miles too far away to offer them a shred of help? Saralynn's parents have always been people with deep faith in the Lord, so they quickly rallied friends and relatives in six states to pray for her safety. And, just as Christ's followers have done through the ages, they turned to the Scriptures for strength and wisdom in those darkest of days. "Since

Thou their God art everywhere, they cannot be where Thou art not," one great old hymn reminds us. Saralynn's parents fastened onto this truth in God's word. In the grand words of the 139th Psalm, for instance, they joined David in praying,

> Where can I go from Your Spirit?
>   Where can I flee from your presence?
> If I go up to the heavens, you are there;
>   if I make my bed in the depths,
>   you are there.
> If I rise on the wings of the dawn,
>   if I settle on the far side of the sea,
> even there your hand will guide me,
>   your right hand will hold me fast.

Words like this bolstered the faith of these good people and reassured them that they were not just wistfully dreaming when they dared to hope that God could shelter their loved ones.

In whatever difficulty they might face.

Wherever they might be.

"Can anyone hide in secret places so that I cannot see him?" declares the LORD. *"Do not I fill heaven and earth?" declares the* LORD. Saralynn's parents rejoiced when they found these words in Jeremiah 23:24. Her mother recalled the proverb that says, *"The eyes of the* LORD *are everywhere, keeping watch on the wicked and the good"* (15:3). When she quoted those words, they spoke instantly to their hearts, assuring them that God's surveillance was much too good for Bert to able to elude him, and his love was too great for Saralynn's little family to be overlooked and forgotten. *"He is not far from each one of us,"* they read together in Acts 17:27. "Surely," they told each other, "that includes our

babies!" In those anxious days, familiar Scriptures shone with new light. Passages like the one where Jesus reminds us that God knows when a sparrow falls and that he keeps count of the hairs on our heads. Or the one where the ancient psalmist rejoiced that the God of heaven doesn't sleep when we do, but watches over his people non-stop.

Don't let me mislead you. Saralynn's parents are realists. They knew only too well the danger their daughter was facing. When a month passed with no word from Saralynn, they told me, "We've been pretty depressed yesterday and today, even though we trust God with the whole thing." Then her mother added with a tearful smile, "*He* knows where they are and *He* will see it through."

* * * * *

I wish I could tell you that this story has a fairy tale happily-ever-after kind of ending. It doesn't. At the time of this writing Saralynn's parents have not heard from her. With each passing month hope dwindles that they ever will. But their trust in the God who loves and sustains us all has not diminished. He is good, even if Bert and all the rogues in the world like him are not. In their mature faith these anguished parents know that we do not love God and serve him because he always gives us what we want and never lets us hurt or cry. "Though he slay me," Job insisted, "yet will I hope in him" (13:15). That's real faith. Faith that keeps on trusting God even when our pain is greatest and the sun refuses to shine. That's when we need to hear the apostle Peter telling us to hold onto the promises of God's word, knowing in our hearts that because he loves us the day indeed will dawn. The morning star will rise.

If not in this life, most certainly when he welcomes us into his eternal glory.

I'm So Lonely

The LORD God said, "It is not good for the man to be alone" (Genesis 2:18).

It had been a frantic week, I recall. Year-end holidays were gearing up. Already we had hosted company at our home, and more family members were on the way soon. So I was working longer hours than usual, pushing harder than usual, making sure I got some deadlined work done early. Before the relatives descended. Before Santa Claus scuttled my usual routines.

I tell you all of this to help you understand my frame of mind when I slipped out of the church study that day and headed to lunch at least an hour later than I had intended to. Feeling the pressure of the duties piling up, I was looking for a quiet place to hide. For a few minutes away from the telephone and the computer. I was hungry, but for more than food. I yearned for some down time. With a good magazine in a quiet cafe booth away from anybody who wanted anything.

So you can imagine how I groaned inside when the gray-haired stranger waiting in the line in front of me at Red Lobster, turned to me without even introducing himself and blurted out, "I'm lonely. Can I eat with you?"

Especially in the Thanksgiving/Christmas season lots of people feel lonely. I suspect that it's not just holiday moodiness. It's a condition of our generation. In so many ways we have polished our skills at protecting our privacy. We have become experts at isolating ourselves. And for this we pay the frightful price of deep, desperate loneliness.

I don't remember ever seeing anyone who looked more forlorn — more lost — than that sad little man who asked to eat with me. His eyes cried out in a frightened but urgent plea for another human being to touch him,

> to look at him,
> > to listen to him,
> > > to laugh with him.

I *did not* want to eat with him! But I couldn't say no. You couldn't have either. Nobody with an ounce of compassion could have told that poor soul to go sit by himself and salt his shrimp dinner with his tears.

"I know you," he said, peering at my face. "I don't know where I've seen you, but I know you."

His memory was better than mine. Cross-referencing our activities for the past two decades, it didn't take us long to came up with a match. Back in the mid-Sixties, during a time when I lived and preached in

Arizona, I had been briefly in Texas preaching a revival for a small church in the north part of town. The local preacher and I had stopped by a warehouse one morning to drink coffee with one of the church leaders. My Red Lobster friend had worked in that warehouse. He had seen me only that one time, years ago. And he remembered!

How awesome, I thought, that God could use such an inconspicuous, commonplace experience to minister to this little man in his time of brokenness and need!

Humbled by the ease with which God had interrupted my selfish plans for the hour, I decided to cry calf-rope to the Almighty. As my new/old friend and I moved toward a booth in the restaurant, I resolved to give myself to him completely for the next hour. (It turned into two.) I would not insult him by offering a few hurried moments and half my mind, grudgingly bestowed. I would give him my full attention. I would be "there" for him as fully as I could.

I owed him that. Because Jesus did the same for me. At a time when Jesus would have much preferred not to, he gave himself totally for me. And every day, when the going is tough for me, he is "there." A Mediator for my prayers. A High Priest who sympathizes with my weaknesses.

Jesus went to the cross for me. This sad little man just wanted me to listen.

Is there some lonely person who needs *you* to listen?

As we started to order our food, I saw for the first time that my elderly friend was at times a bit confused. He wanted to order the Monday shrimp special. It embarrassed him when both the waitress and I assured him it was Thursday. When the waitress failed to hide her impatience with what she obviously saw as "a dumb old man," I saw him wince. She cut his heart.

How easily the young can wound the old — and never know it, I mused to myself. Only a few days before this unplanned encounter, I had run across some startling research proving that symptoms of senility (such as my dinner companion's forgetfulness) can be produced in the young simply by treating them as if they are old.

"Rise up before the old man," the Scriptures admonish us.

"Gray hair is a crown of glory," the Book says.

Today science confirms this ancient wisdom. Our continued expressions of love and esteem protect our aging kin from mental and emotional deterioration. Today we know that loneliness and lack of love are killers.

As we waited for our food, the old-timer began a play-by-play account of his last two years. Or maybe I should describe it as a pain-by-pain account. He had suffered two heart attacks in the past two years. Which he described in the kind of minute detail our minds retain only in reference to our own ailments. A year ago he had been through heart bypass surgery at a local hospital.

I thought back to this conversation recently when I read the results of a University of California medical research team. After a year's study they concluded, "Loneliness has a greater impact on the death rate than smoking, drinking, eating, and exercise." That's heavy, people!

It's dangerous to play Elijah for long. Remember Elijah? He was the Old Testament prophet who retreated from humanity into a desert cave. In modern parlance we'd say, "He dug a hole and pulled it in on top of himself." And down there in that lonely lair he wailed to God, "I, only I am left. I'm all alone, the only faithful prophet alive, and they're trying to kill me!"

Elijah wound up lonely because of depression. Or, is it possible, he wound up depressed because he chose to be lonely? The latter may be truer. Maybe depression was able to overtake old Elijah because he got his theology all mixed up and began to think the success and survival of God's work depended on him and not on God. That's always a damaging viewpoint.

If we study the story in 1 Kings 19, we can see that Elijah's loneliness was largely self-imposed. As is so often true. Sometimes it's hard for those of us who are lonely to see it, but we often do things to alienate others and to isolate ourselves.

I've known parents who drove their kids away. And then spent years feeling lonely.

I've known church members who created all sorts of barriers between themselves and the other members of the congregation. They wouldn't let anybody get close to them. For years they have belonged to the church, at least officially. But, by choice, they're all alone.

Some of the loneliest people I know are young people. College students miles away from mama for the first time. High school kids, who have been moved by their parents to a town where they know nobody. In September they find themselves in a huge school building cram-packed full of other kids who are strangers, so they live in a private shell of misery. Could this be one

reason that the leading cause of death among high
school and college students is suicide?

At a retreat at Laity Lodge some years ago, Professor
Bruce Coryell shared with us his hurt at losing his wife
less than a year before. "I'm in the highest danger cate-
gory for a heart attack," he said. "I'm a widower, over
40, in the first year of grief." He knew the danger of
loneliness.

"It is not good for man to be alone."

My talkative friend in the restaurant spoke about his
wife: how much she had helped him during his sick-
ness and how much he loved her. Then, as our meal-
time dragged on, I noted that for the first time in our
conversation he began to refer to her in the past tense. It
never seemed to dawn on him that he had not told me
she was gone.

Before long I found out why he avoided the subject.
His wife was dead because six months ago, on their first
auto trip after his heart surgery, he had fallen asleep at
the wheel and hit a guard rail, rolling their new car. She
died instantly, the coroner said.

But I found out, as I talked to her grieving husband,
that she was not dead at all. She haunted every movement of his mind. Not only was there the obvious,
devastating guilt because his mistake had killed her. He
had plenty of that guilt. But he was also tormented by a
far worse guilt — guilt that tortured him because of the
way he felt about her before she died.

For six or seven years, he told me, his wife's health
had been so bad that they had enjoyed no intimate rela-
tions. During the final year or so, she had accused him
of being unfaithful to her. "No normal man would go

this long without sex," she bitterly blamed him. "You haven't been sleeping with me, so I know you've been in bed with somebody!" He protested his innocence, but to the day she died she refused to believe him.

The loneliness of this widower began a long time before his wife's funeral. And her death added a cruel twist to it.

Seldom have I seen a young man eat as much shrimp as my dinner partner put away that day. We talked almost two hours. He ate heartily, and talked non-stop the whole time.

Out of politeness, and with absolutely no desire to open another can of worms, I asked during one of the rare lulls in the conversation if he had children. He sounded so lonely that I wondered how he possibly could. Unfortunately I found out!

He was just confused enough, and I was just enough ignorant of his family's make-up that I never did completely sort out all the raunchy details. But somehow this meek, quiet, vulnerable, lovable little man had made one of his sons so angry that the boy had not talked to his father in seven years. The old man wept as he tried to explain all this to me, but he turned too many blind corners without warning for me to follow the thread of his tale.

I was afraid to ask any more questions. Two hours had passed and I needed to be gone. Also, I knew it was not good counseling practice to abandon a person with all their worms out of the can. And by now we had a whole swarm of them crawling around. Every innocent question I had asked the old gentleman had produced another heartbreaking revelation of another broken relationship.

Here he was somewhere in his mid-seventies, and every person who should have been standing by him to love and encourage and care was, instead, at odds with him.

And he was lonely.

What did I have to offer this lonely stranger?
My attention and concern.
My time.
My Lord.

I longed for another time, on a better day, when I could help this lonely soul find the companionship he craves and the encouragement he's dying for in the Nazarene I serve.

I'm convinced that this man, in the toughest days of his life, needs to see Jesus in Gethsemane, and hear him asking his men, "Could you not watch with me? Don't you know that right now I need your friendship?" If my lonely friend sees this vignette of Jesus, he will know at least that Jesus understands his distress.

At a time when his family has slandered and rejected him, my dinner companion needs to see in the Bible that when Jesus came to his own family, "his own received him not." In fact, his brothers called him crazy. So he understands.

After more than 70 years, the man in the restaurant did not really know where home was. Surely it would help him to hear the sadness in Jesus' voice as he said, "Foxes have holes and birds of the air have nests, but I don't have a home. The Son of man has no place to lay his head."

That day the man I ate with at Red Lobster was far too confused, his thoughts much too scrambled, for me to tell him all this. But, if you're drowning in loneliness today, I recommend that you go back and read the last three paragraphs. Focus on the sure truth that Jesus knows what it means to be alone, rejected, and left out. He knows, and he cares when we're lonely.

The Mystery of Love

Husbands, love your wives, just as Christ loved the church and gave himself up for her (Ephesians 5:25).

I first became aware of the name of Robertson McQuilkin when he began to write occasional columns for *Christianity Today*. Quickly I learned to look forward to anything from his pen. He wrote with good humor and keen insight. I liked his stuff.

But I like even more his extraordinary life in the years that have followed.

In the fall of 1990 Dr. McQuilkin shocked the evangelical Christian world by unexpectedly resigning as president of Columbia Bible College and Seminary in South Carolina (now Columbia International University). Although his board had known his intentions for some time, the Christian public was blindsided by the announcement of Dr. McQuilkin's early retirement. He was a rising star in Christian education and journalism. Already he had written a blockbuster book on Christian ethics from a biblical perspective. Here was a man destined to leave his positive mark on the face of conservative Christian efforts in our generation.

Dr. McQuilkin's departure from Columbia's helm stunned many who knew him, but his reason for leaving did not surprise them. His wife needed him, he told the supporters of the school. He explained that his lovely lady, Muriel, had been diagnosed with Alzheimer's. Already this silent destroyer had been at work on Muriel for more than ten years, McQuilkin revealed. Now the disease had disabled her so much that she needed constant attention. So this good man, at the pinnacle of his career, stepped down and turned over the governance of his school to another. Backers of the school begged him to reconsider. His answer was appreciative but firm. "My wife needs me more than the school does," he said. "The school can find another president who will lead it well. Muriel has no husband but me."

Back in October, 1990, as I read the brief article this good man wrote to explain his decision, I got goose bumps. Literally. In an age so accustomed to worshiping Success, here was a Christian man who recognized a higher value. He turned his back on honor and acclaim in public Christian service to keep his marriage vows. To do his duty. I don't mind telling you that I was impressed.

Soon Robertson McQuilkin faded from the limelight of Christian leadership circles. His name no longer appeared on the school stationery. His byline no longer graced the big-name magazines. Except for a small circle of relatives and friends in Columbia, this man who had seemed destined for greatness dropped from sight. Or, perhaps I should say, he ascended to a nobler level of greatness. For over five years now he has provided constant daily care for Muriel. While friends marvel at his patient acceptance of such a distasteful role, he offers a different perspective on their circumstance. "In her silent world," McQuilkin writes, "Muriel is so content, so lovable." Losing her would not be a welcome relief, he insists. "If Jesus took her home," he says, "how I would miss her gentle, sweet presence."

By this he does not imply that his task is all sweetness and light. With his typical good humor McQuilkin tells of a time, back in the days when Muriel could still walk and before they resorted to diapers, when he was trying to clean up an "accident" she had. And Muriel, always the one who cleaned up messes in better days, insisted on trying to help him. But with hands that no longer knew what to do or how to do it. McQuilkin says, "I mopped frantically, trying to fend off the interfering hands, and contemplated how best to get a soiled slip over a head that was totally opposed to the idea. At that moment Chuck Swindoll boomed over the radio in the kitchen, 'Men! Are you at home? *Really* at home?'" McQuilkin says, "In the midst of my stinking immersion I smiled, 'Yeah, Chuck, I really am.'"

Why would a dignified, highly educated, widely respected man subject himself to such indignity? He says the reason is simple. "I love her." By the world's definition love is an ephemeral feeling that evaporates if the relationship stops being fun. Or physical. Or mutual. Good communication and satisfying sex and shared duties are heralded by modern gurus as the essentials for a happy marriage. Take these away and what's left? Today Muriel McQuilkin has almost nothing left to contribute to her marriage. She can't walk, or talk, or feed herself, or read a book. She's unable to attend to her slightest bodily need. Yet, mysteriously, her husband still loves her.

Like all family members of Alzheimer's patients, McQuilkin has read all the literature and reached out to many available resources to learn how best to deal with Muriel's plight. "I attended a workshop in which an expert told us that there were two reasons people keep a family member at home rather than in a nursing facility: economic necessity or feelings of guilt. Afterwards," McQuilkin says, "I spoke with her privately, trying to elicit some other possible motive for keeping someone at home. But she insisted those were the only two motives. Finally I asked, 'What about love?' 'Oh,' she replied, 'we put that under guilt.'" Reflecting on this incident later, McQuilkin shrugs, "So much for love."

But this man's love for his wife, so mysterious and even unbelievable to those who order their lives on different priorities, is the only way to explain their ongoing relationship. A college freshman once asked Dr. McQuilkin if he missed being college president. His amazing answer was that he'd never thought about it. Supplying Muriel's care seemed so obvious a mandate that he walked away from his office and never looked back. Hooked by this student's question, however, McQuilkin says he had trouble sleeping that night. He prayed, "Father, I like this assignment, and I have no regrets. But if a coach puts a man on the bench, he must not want him in the game. You needn't tell me, of course, but I'd like to know — why don't you need me in the game?"

The next morning they were walking, he and Muriel. She was still unsteadily mobile in those days, so they were slowly navigating around their block, holding hands both for love and stability, when a local derelict staggered past them. "Tha's good. I likes 'at," the bum chanted with a drunken smile. "Tha's real good," he repeated. "I likes it." And he gamboled on down the street, mumbling that distorted phrase to himself over and over. Back in the safety of their little garden, McQuilkin sat down beside Muriel, when the inebriated words of the derelict came back to him. And he heard them anew, this time as God's answer to his prayer, His message to his spirit. "I like it. Tha's good." And that's really all that matters, McQuilkin submits: what God likes.

How does Robertson McQuilkin hold up under the emotion and physical drain that has undone so many Alzheimer's caregivers? "Right now," he says somewhat astoundingly, "I think my life must be happier than the lives of 95 percent of the people on planet Earth. Muriel's a joy to me." But, he admits, it has not all been easy. Two years before he quit his job at the college, a tragic accident snatched away his oldest son. That burden of grief, added to the anguish of Muriel's steady decline, banished joy from his life. "My faith could better be described as resignation," he writes about those hard days. Only by willfully concentrating on the Cross, only by focusing doggedly on how much Jesus suffered for him, could McQuilkin hold on to the assurance that God loves him regardless of present burdens and sorrows. In those dark days, doubt gnawed at him.

"Then," he says, "I remembered the secret I had learned in younger days — going to a mountain hideaway to be alone with God." There, with some difficulty he confides, he was able slowly to break the ruinous habit of dwelling on his own hurts and thus managed to set his soul free to gaze once more at Jesus. "When that happened," he recalls, "I learned what God had taught me more than once before: *the heavy heart lifts on wings of praise.*"

McQuilkin's inventory of resources for coping with Muriel's disease include not only his rekindled faith, but his family and his friends. And memories. Especially helpful to him, he says, are his memories of the times they laughed together. "Sometimes," he concedes, "the happy doesn't bubble up with joy but rains down gently with tears." To validate this, he recalls a line from the stage version of *Shadowlands,* when C.S. Lewis tells his wife that he doesn't want to think about the fact that their joyful togetherness will soon end, and she replies, "The pain is part of the happiness. That's the deal."

It is, of course. For all of us. There is no such thing as a parent without tears. Nor can anyone imagine belonging to the church without sharing in her sorrows. We are truly a part of any group — a faculty, or a football team, or firefighting squad, or a Weigh Down chapter — only when we're willing to shoulder our share of the heartache as well as the glory. Nothing that matters in this life can be ours pain-free. "Pain is part of the happiness. That's the deal."

But the pain of Alzheimer's has an insidious way of wounding caregivers in relentlessly minute ways.

Muriel's right hand went limp not long ago. It was her first major physical loss since she became unable to stand or to feed herself about a year and a half before. "A little loss, you would think, but I shed a few tears," McQuilkin chronicles. That night he wrote in his journal, "It's almost like part of me dies with each of her little deaths." He remembered how creative that hand was. How loving. How busy it had been for him and for others. The loss was particularly poignant because it had been her last means of communication. She would grasp his hand, he says, or pat him on the back when he hugged her, or even push him away when she objected to something he was doing for her. So he writes, "I miss her hand."

I suppose this would not be true for husbands and wives who never make time to converse with one another, but for Dr. McQuilkin, one way of coping with Muriel's mental and emotional absence is to replay in his mind little snippets of conversations they shared in better days. "I don't know everything?" she fired back at him one day long ago. "Why, I know *more* than everything. I know some things that aren't so!" One night right before they went to sleep, he was winning an argument with what he and most other masculine types would call "irresistible logic." In his memory (and I paraphrase his own words to describe that instant) he can still see her rise up on one elbow and transfix him with fire in her grey-green eyes as she says to him, "Well, let me tell you something. Logic's not everything, and feeling's not nothing." Memories like that fill huge gaps. "In the uninterrupted silences of today," Dr. McQuilkin writes, "the memories of sweet and spicy talk long gone bring pleasure once again."

Almost all Alzheimer's specialists agree that the
disease they treat and study is one of the cruelest
known to humanity, but the victim in Alzheimer's is
not the patient, they say. It's the caregiver. Reflecting on
this oft-repeated observation, Robertson McQuilkin
says he wondered why he never felt like a victim. In his
journal on Valentine's Day, 1995, he wrote that night,
"The reason I don't feel like a victim is — I'm not!"
From time to time associates urge him to "call it quits,"
to find alternative care for Muriel. He responds, "Do
you realize how lonely I would be without her?"

Knowledgeable as he is about the horrors of
Alzheimer's disease, surely Dr. McQuilkin would be the
first person to admit that he and Muriel have been
blessed beyond measure by the fact they have been
spared the anger and abusiveness the disease often
spawns in its victims. They have been allowed what he
sees as good years together, where others have not been
given that option. In telling the McQuilkins' story, I do
not mean to heap pain and guilt on Alzheimer's caregivers whose loved ones have been unmanageable at
home. I simply mean to celebrate with this grand
Christian couple the victory of their faith and love
against unthinkable odds.

Months, even years, have passed since Muriel spoke a
sentence or held anything like a conversation. Even coher-
ent single words have vanished now. So the experience
they had on that 1995 Valentine's Day is one McQuilkin
won't forget. Valentine's Day always has been special in
their home, he explains, because on that day in 1948
Muriel agreed to marry him. Let him tell you in his own
words what happened on that special day 47 years later:

After I bathed Muriel on her bed that Valentine's eve and kissed her good night (she still enjoys two things: good food and kissing!), I whispered a prayer over her: "Dear Jesus, you love sweet Muriel more than I, so please keep my beloved through the night; may she hear the angel choirs."

The next morning I was peddling on my Exercycle at the foot of her bed and reminiscing about some of our happy lovers' days long gone while Muriel slowly emerged from sleep. Finally, she popped awake and, as she often does, smiled at me. Then, for the first time in months she spoke, calling out to me in a voice clear as a crystal chime, "Love. . .love. . .love." I jumped from my cycle and ran to embrace her. "Honey, you really do love me, don't you?" Holding me with her eyes and patting my back, she responded with the only words she could find to say yes: "I'm nice," she said.

Those may prove to be the last words she ever spoke.

Business leader Fred Smith tells about stopping one day at a doughnut shop in Grand Saline, Texas. He says a young farm couple were sitting at a table next to his. The man was wearing overalls, as you might expect. The lady had on a fresh gingham dress. When the couple finished their doughnuts, the husband got up to pay their bill. Fred noticed that the woman didn't get up to follow him.

When the farmer came back, he stood in front of his wife. She put her arms around his neck and he lifted her up. Only then did Fred see that she was wearing a full-body brace. Slowly her husband lifted her up out of her chair. Then Fred says the man backed out of the front door to their pickup truck, with his wife all the time hanging from his neck.

Gently the fellow hoisted her into the truck. All the chatter in the doughnut shop stopped while every eye watched this little drama. As the farm couple drove away, nobody said anything until one waitress remarked, "Man! He took his vows seriously!"

So did Robertson McQuilkin.

Husbands, love your wives, just as Christ loved the church and gave himself up for her.

Gene Shelburne wears an amazing assortment of hats, serving this hour as a columnist, the next as a maker of sermons, and another as a doting grandfather. As each day passes, he adroitly shifts roles, starting each school day in a public high school classroom teaching Bible, spending part of each day chairing boards for various community-based Christian projects, and somehow finding time in between all this to write books like the one you hold in your hand. For 29 years he has served as pulpit minister of the Anna Street Church in Amarillo, Texas. His column, *Cross Currents*, runs in the Amarillo *Daily News* and in several other newspapers. His previous book, *The God Who Puts Us Back Together*, has been a bestseller for College Press. For 38 years, Gene says, he has been loving Anita, and they proudly claim a daughter, two sons, and ten splendid grandchildren.